DEAD
OR ALIVE?

Hello

DEAD OR ALIVE?

Hello

The truth and relevance of Jesus' resurrection

Daniel Clark
foreword by Rico Tice

ivp

INTER-VARSITY PRESS
Norton Street, Nottingham NG7 3HR, England
Email: ivp@ivpbooks.com
Website: www.ivpbooks.com

First published 2007

British Library Cataloguing in Publication Data
A catalogue record for this book is available from the British Library.

ISBN-10: 1–84474–156–7
ISBN-13: 978–1–84474–156–4

Illustrations © Richard Jones
Typeset in Dante 10.5/13pt by CRB Associates, Reepham, Norfolk, UK
Printed by Ashford Colour Press Ltd, Gosport, Hampshire, UK

Inter-Varsity Press publishes Christian books that are true to the Bible and that
communicate the gospel, develop discipleship and strengthen the church for its
mission in the world.

Inter-Varsity Press is closely linked with the Universities and Colleges Christian
Fellowship, a student movement connecting Christian Unions in universities and
colleges throughout Great Britain, and a member movement of the International
Fellowship of Evangelical Students. Website: www.uccf.org.uk

Contents

Part 2: Is it true?

Part 3: So what?

Acknowledgments

Many people have helped in various different ways to bring this book to print. You know who you are – thank you all. Doubtless some reading this will recognize the occasional turn of phrase or idea as theirs – thanks to you, too!

This book is dedicated, with gratitude, to my grandparents. Two are still serving faithfully, two have 'fallen asleep'; all have prayed consistently for me. Their trust in Jesus springs from his death; their hope for the future from Jesus' resurrection. 1 Thessalonians 4.14–18.

A brief guide to Bible references used in this book

The Bible isn't one long book but a library of sixty-six different books, written in several different languages by many authors over thousands of years.

References to quotes from the Bible come in the form: book chapter.verse(s). So Matthew 28.1–10 refers to the book of Matthew, chapter 28, verses 1 to 10. Where multiple references come from the same book, they are separated by a semi-colon. For example, Luke 16.19–31; 19.1–10 refers to the book of Luke, chapter 16 verses 19 to 31 and chapter 19 verses 1 to 10. Multiple references with the same chapter are separated by a comma. For example, Luke 24.25–27, 44–47 refers to the book of Luke, chapter 24, verses 25 to 27 and 44 to 47.

There are various different English translations of the Bible, some opting for a more literal translation of the original text; others for a more colloquial translation, known as paraphrasing. Most of the time, I quote from the New International Version (NIV), the most widely-used translation of the Bible in the UK. On occasion, I have used a paraphrase such as The Message or the Contemporary English Version (CEV). I have tried to make quotes gender-inclusive where the original text allows it, even if the published translation retains a male bias.

Foreword

As I put pen to paper it's Easter Saturday and I have just returned with a heavy heart from purchasing a paper at my local newsagents.

Naturally at this time of the year the resurrection is at the forefront of my mind. So I looked along the paper rack to see if there was any mention of Easter Day, let alone its significance. Strikingly, the only acknowledgment of this central Christian festival was on the front of a tabloid which read as follows: 'Easter Miracle, face of Jesus found on a boiled egg', with the command 'Thou shalt not eat, says Mum'. Apparently a Colorado mother named Linda Bargas is claiming an Easter miracle after some dye she coloured onto a boiled egg dried and transformed itself into the face of Jesus. The message from the news-stand was pretty stark. Easter has nothing to say to the real world of terrorism, fuel prices, family break-up, party conferences and debt. No, actually its only part in the news is to provide some weird entertainment to a smirking tabloid.

By contrast I have found *Dead or Alive?* a fine response. Not least because some of the changed lives it depicts would merit a column in any objective newspaper.

By any standard it is pretty compelling to read about Slobodan, who fought in the Yugoslav army, lost his mother and brother in car and work accidents respectively and first heard about Christ while in a psychiatric hospital. By any standard it is pretty compelling to read of Terry, the first hooligan to be charged with manslaughter after the 1985 Heysel Stadium tragedy, who after his prison sentence and conversion went to Juventus to seek forgiveness from the bereaved families. By any standard it is pretty compelling to read of Darren living with cerebral palsy and writing, 'As a Christian I believe and trust in a God who has suffered. God understands my suffering and loves me unconditionally.'

And if these are the headline-grabbing stories in the book, what are the facts behind them? For example how can Christine, age forty-five, with inoperable terminal cancer, claim, 'With faith it's possible to live with it.' How is all this substantiated? Well, I'm delighted to report that Daniel Clark gives the honest searcher and indeed the cynical sceptic a great deal of compelling material to consider. As one author acknowledges, 'The very stubbornness of the facts themselves' are laid out.

Actually there were times when Daniel Clark reminded me of Doctor Luke, who at the start of his Gospel claims, 'I myself have carefully investigated everything from the beginning', Luke 1.3. And not only has the biblical evidence been sifted, the contemporary critics are given some real airtime. For example I found the material on *The Da Vinci Code* particularly striking and will now sound much more informed when asked about the assertions of Sir Leigh Teabing.

It all adds up to the fact that I am confronted by the resurrection as an unavoidable issue. Jesus Christ cannot be relegated to the world of the nursery, make-believe and coloured eggs. No. Any rounded debate on suffering, death, religion and meaning has to include this evidence and I loved the way the last line of various chapters made that clear:

'If he's now lying in a grave, he can't help us find answers to our questions.'

'We're left not only with our questions, but also our pain.'

'How exactly can Jesus make us alive?'

Rico Tice
Associate Minister, All Souls Church, Langham Place, London

Introduction: Why read a book about Jesus' resurrection?

He was born in an obscure village, the unwanted, unexpected child of an unmarried peasant woman. He was a manual labourer until he was thirty. Then for three years he was an itinerant preacher and miracle-worker. Thousands were captivated by his teaching, and flocked to hear him. His biographers tell us that in the days before modern medicine, he healed many with a word or a touch, and sick people were carried for miles just to come into his presence.

He was never elected to power; nor did he have spin-doctors to steer international media in his favour. He didn't go to university, have formal qualifications or travel to the leading cities of the world. He did none of the things usually associated with greatness. He had no credentials but himself.

He was only thirty-three when the tide of public opinion turned against him: his friends evaporated, and the masses bayed for his death. His hands and feet were nailed to wooden beams, and he was left hanging to die between two common criminals. While he was dying, his executioners gambled for his clothes, the only property he had.

Twenty centuries have come and gone, yet he is more famous and popular than anyone who has ever lived. All the armies that ever fought, all the air forces that ever bombed, all the parliaments that ever sat, all the presidents and monarchs that ever ruled, put together, have not affected the life of men and women on this earth as much as that one solitary life.[1]

Why look at *Jesus*?

Although he lived two thousand years ago, Jesus' character towers over the pages of human history. Great leaders such as George Washington and Napoleon Bonaparte are still remembered a few hundred years later; one imagines that people like Albert Einstein and Martin Luther King will still be hailed for a few centuries yet. But who else has their birth celebrated as a national holiday in almost two hundred countries in every corner of the planet two thousand years later?

Today, more than two billion people – one third of the world's population – claim to follow Jesus Christ. His birth marks the start of the Western calendar; his teaching underpins our legal justice system; remembrance of his death shapes our academic terms. Faith in him has inspired ordinary individuals to great goals: the explorer Sir Francis Drake, the scientist Sir Isaac Newton, the civil rights activist Martin Luther King and the humanitarian worker Mother Teresa – to name but a few – took their lead from Jesus.

Yet despite his obvious greatness and our society's current resurgence of interest in all things spiritual, there is also an increasing ignorance about Jesus – a fact innocently epitomized by a boy who recently asked why Jesus, the founder of Christianity, was named after a swear word. Many people discard a belief in Jesus at the same time as they grow out of believing in Father Christmas, and never – as adults – think seriously about the most influential man who's ever lived. Have you?

Why look at Jesus' *resurrection*?

If Jesus' life stands far above all others in human history, his resurrection – his bodily coming back to life having been publicly executed – must rank as the single biggest event in world history. No war or natural disaster has had such widespread, long-term effects. If Jesus had stayed in the grave after his crucifixion on that first Good Friday, the world would have forgotten about him long ago. At best he would feature as a footnote in history books under a section on Roman emperors ('For three years, an itinerant preacher called Jesus attracted a large following in modern-day Israel, but his fledgling movement soon evaporated after he was brutally executed').

Jesus' resurrection is absolutely central to the Christian faith. One of the first Christian leaders wrote:

> If Christ wasn't raised to life, our message is worthless, and so is your faith. If the dead won't be raised to life, we have told lies about God by saying that he raised Christ to life, when he really did not . . . Unless Christ was raised to life, your faith is useless, and you are still living in your sins. And those people who died after putting their faith in him are completely lost. If our hope in Christ is good only for this life, we are worse off than anyone else.[2]

In other words, if the resurrection foundation is removed, the whole edifice of Christianity collapses into a pile of dust: Christian preaching is useless; Christian faith is futile; the Christian claim of forgiveness for the past is rendered void; the Christian hope of heaven is make-believe.

So here's my tip: the quickest way to weigh-up whether or not Jesus has anything to offer our world is by examining his resurrection. If the claims about his coming back to life are grossly exaggerated, you can knock Christianity off your list of genuine spiritual options straight away. But if it's true, then it shows us that there is a real spiritual power at work in the world that we can tap into.

Have you ever looked carefully at the evidence surrounding Jesus' resurrection?

Why should *I* look at Jesus' resurrection?

I haven't written this book to waste your time. At the moment you might think that whether or not Jesus was raised from the dead is about as relevant as the current weather forecast on Mars. But I've discovered that Jesus' resurrection is the basis of fantastic news for me here and now – news far too good to keep to myself. Millions of others around the world have come to that same realization and have committed themselves to following the risen Jesus. In fact, from the very earliest days of the Christian faith, it's been heralded as 'the *good news* about Jesus and the resurrection' – news which is 'for you and your children and for all who are far off'.[3] Wouldn't you like to get some good news?

What's more, Jesus' resurrection sheds light on some of the big questions we all ask – questions about life, death, God and meaning. In part 1 of this book, we'll explore those very questions in the light of Jesus' resurrection. In part 2, we'll look at the evidence for Jesus' resurrection itself, so that you can come to your own informed conclusion about whether or not Jesus did come back from beyond the grave, never to die again. Part 3 will unpack exactly why Jesus and his resurrection is such good news for us personally.

But above all, I don't simply want to persuade you that Jesus' resurrection is relevant and true – after all, our world isn't interested in pious-sounding theory. Jesus claimed that he came to offer us 'life to the full', so I want to show you that following the risen Jesus is life-transforming *in practice*. Throughout this book, I'll introduce you to a handful of Jesus' followers. I've deliberately chosen people from many different backgrounds and walks of life around the world, because if Jesus really *does* offer life to the full, then it must be able to work for anyone and everyone. Meeting these ordinary people is a way for you to judge whether following the risen Jesus actually *works*.

Over to you

Don't you owe it to yourself to explore the evidence and implications of history's greatest single event – especially because if it's true, it's good news for you personally?

real lives

Sally

Sally Phillips is a comedy actress who co-created the Emmy-award winning 'Smack the Pony' and featured in the Bridget Jones films. More recently, she has appeared in 'Green Wing' and 'Jam and Jerusalem'. She lives in London.

Sally, how did you become a Christian, and what difference has it made?

By the time I left university, I was incredibly irreligious. I did a show at the Edinburgh festival called 'Jesus II: He's back from the dead, he's cross, he's everywhere and he wants your soul'. We had a picture of Jesus on the programme cover holding a machine gun. I was very happy with my anti-Christian stance, I felt all Christians wore bad clothes, didn't think things through and were very smug.

Four years later, I started researching a sitcom about witches. Then I started getting very bad nightmares. Working in a very un-Christian environment, it was impossible to tell someone about my religious trauma. I'd stand outside bookshops wondering how embarrassing it would be to buy a Bible.

Unusually, I worked with two Christians at a sitcom festival: an actor who was very overt with his faith, and a stand-up who was very private. Six weeks of heated debates later, the actor prayed for me at 3 am in Hammersmith shopping centre, and I became a Christian. I felt pretty isolated until the stand-up pointed me to a church where I could make close friends. That church is still home.

Trying to turn my life around was (and remains) hard work. The 'lie amnesty' of '96 was particularly excruciating. Things have definitely changed. Before I became a Christian, my writing was quite unhealthy – full of things I was angry and hurt about. Since I've become a Christian I've done simple characters who are slightly in trouble all the time, but mean well. That's how I experience my Christian walk.

At the beginning I had people shouting at me because they were frightened that I'd judge them, and frightened that it's true. Recently I've really sensed a change – perhaps because I'm more confident in my own faith and denying Jesus less!

part one

Is it relevant?

Can Jesus' resurrection help us find
answers to the big questions in life?

1. Is there anybody out there?

At some point in our lives, all of us begin to ask big questions. When we are waiting for yet another late-running bus, or putting in the umpteenth load of washing for the week, we wonder whether there's more to this life than tedious routine. When a friend's life is turned upside down by accident or illness, we ask

why there's so much suffering in the world. When a relative dies, we ponder what will happen when we die.

These are the sorts of questions we'll be looking at in these first chapters:

- Questions about purpose: what is the point of life?
- Questions about destiny: what happens when we die?
- Questions about suffering: why is there so much in our world?
- Questions about god: does he/she/it exist? If so, what is he/she/it like?

Often, these questions give us a headache if we consider them for too long, so we just press on with life before discovering any answers. Or the bus suddenly turns up, and we forget that the question even began to form in our mind. Sometimes we reject the questions, because we're scared of the answers we might discover. Or we simply give up asking because we're not finding any answers. Life does not always make much sense, and that not only hurts us, but it disappoints us as well. Deep down, we know we would love to find some answers.

Life does not always make much sense, and that not only hurts us, but it disappoints us as well.

Is there a key that will help us unlock some answers? My conviction is that Jesus – and in particular, his resurrection – is a key that helps to unlock some answers to life's big questions. At first sight, it's an unlikely-looking key – two thousand years old, and made in a place and culture far removed from our own. Yet the big questions we ask aren't new ones: ever since *homo sapiens* existed, people have been asking them. So an ancient key from far away shouldn't necessarily be discarded out of hand. Besides, if we really want to unlock some answers to these questions, isn't any key worth trying?

You may not believe that Jesus lived, died or really did come back from the dead – in other words, that the key doesn't even exist! But for the time being, I'd like to invite you to imagine: 'Just *suppose* that Jesus' resurrection *is* true . . .' If it helps us make sense of life, it'll certainly be worth investigating the historicity of Jesus' life, death and resurrection – which is what we'll do thoroughly in part 2. In the meantime, let's see if the key fits . . .

Searching for the Other

Have you ever had your breath taken away by nature's beauty? I can vividly remember driving through a mountain range, struggling to keep my eyes on the road, because I desperately wanted to soak in the majesty of the views around! On another occasion, I was overwhelmed when I glimpsed the stunning colours and intricate design of underwater coral. At moments like these, words are deeply inadequate, and even our holiday photos are pale reminders of the experience. We're rendered speechless with awe; our spirits somehow seem to be lifted onto a higher plane. Some people talk about a feeling of the numinous – being filled with a sense of a supernatural presence.

For other people, the experience can be a bit different. For many, holding their new-born child can only be described as 'a miracle' or 'a spiritual moment'. Even those who call themselves agnostics – not sure whether or not there is a god – would agree that it is experiences like these which make them think twice about the supernatural realm.

Opinion polls in the UK report that about 70% of the population believe in a god of some sort or another, but there is increasing uncertainty about what such a god is like. A comedian was once asked what he thought about God. 'I don't know,' he quipped. 'We've never been properly introduced.' Spike Milligan was asked if he ever prayed. 'Yes,' he said, 'I pray desperately, all the time: get me out of this mess. But I don't know who I'm praying to.'

Despite this uncertainty, interest in 'spirituality' is growing fast. In our increasingly frenetic and stressful world, more and more people are recognizing that they need some source for energy and strength in order to cope with life's demands, and an inner peace to help them relax. Many are looking to alternative or Eastern views of the gods for inspiration. Some look to 'Mother Earth'. Others look to 'the god in me'.

But even these spiritualities provide little certainty. Madonna has said that 'Everyone has their own god', and that she turns to hers 'to rise above everyday life and the things that bring you down, and mortality and things like that.' However, when asked to describe her god more closely, she replied, 'You know I really have unformed ideas about it because I could change my mind in about half an hour.'[1]

Many of us *think* there is someone out there, and at heart, most of us *hope* that there is, but if we are honest, our best guesses are

still stabs in the dark. Our question remains: Is there anybody out there? If so, what is he/she/it like? Indeed, how can we find out?

What if God were one of us?

Suppose a girl from a rural part of Africa is brought to England on a special trip. She's heard about the Queen, but as she's never had access to a television, she's no idea what the Queen's like. The girl and her guide make their way to Buckingham Palace, with the girl full of questions: 'What's her hair like – is it long and blonde? And how big is she – is she really big?' (After all, in some parts of Africa, it's considered good to be fat.) As they get to Buckingham Palace, she sees one of the Household Guards standing guard. 'Wow – does the Queen wear a uniform like that, too?' she asks, pointing at their red jackets and tall, furry black hats.

The girl is so excited to be at the Queen's home that she jumps up and down and waves her arms, shouting out to the Queen, trying to encourage her to come out. Eventually, one of the Guards takes pity on her and says, 'I'm sorry, miss, but the Queen's busy at the moment. But you can stand here and have your photo taken with me if you want.' The girl is devastated, and nothing can console her. In fact, she becomes convinced that the Queen doesn't even exist at all – and not even going to the postcard stand and looking at pictures of the Queen persuades her. She and her guide go and feed the ducks in the park instead.

Of course, what that girl really needed was for the Queen to come out onto her balcony and wave at her – or better still, to stroll outside onto the Mall and chat with her, even to go and feed the ducks with her.

Sometimes, we can be like that child, trying to guess what god is like. It can be fun guessing, and our guesses can be very sincere and even strongly-held, but at the end of the day, what we really need is for god (if there is such a thing) to make itself known. If it doesn't do that, it's easy to conclude that god doesn't exist.

The Christian claim is that despite living in heaven, God has come down into the real world, walking and talking with real humans. God has chosen to make himself known in a way which we can understand. Joan Osborne's famous hit song 'What if God was one of us' asked, 'If God had a name, what would it be? If God had a face, what would it look like?' If we'd been alive in Israel two thousand years ago, we could have seen God face to face in the person of Jesus – and we could have found out what he's like. It's a staggering claim, so what is it about Jesus' life, teaching and resurrection that can substantiate it? Can he satisfy our searching for the Other, providing a permanent point of reference in a swirling sea of best guesses?

If we'd been alive in Israel two thousand years ago, we could have seen God face to face in the person of Jesus.

Jesus' life and teaching gives evidence of a supernatural power

Anyone who reads one of the four earliest surviving biographies of Jesus (known as the 'gospels') will know that Jesus was an extraordinary man, and virtually everyone agrees that he had access to a supernatural power, which was seen in many ways. For example:

Jesus' teaching. Jesus' moral, ethical and spiritual teaching left the crowds 'amazed … because he taught them as one who had authority', unlike the religious experts of his day.[2] Muhammad, Gandhi, the Dalai Lama and all the great spiritual leaders since Jesus have applauded his teaching, and encouraged others to follow it. Even some great non-religious leaders have adopted Jesus' principles.

Jesus' power to heal. Doctors today can heal many diseases with the aid of sophisticated medical treatments. By contrast, Jesus healed people with just a touch of the hand or word of command. After one such healing of a paralysed man, who 'got up, took his mat and walked out in full view of them all', one of Jesus' biographers records that 'this amazed everyone and they praised God, saying, "We have never seen anything like this!"'[3] The gospels even record occasions where people who had died were brought back to life at his command. Not surprisingly, 'At this, the [crowds] were completely astonished.'[4]

Jesus' power over nature. Meteorologists can sometimes forecast when storms are going to occur, but they cannot stop them happening. In a boat being tossed about on a stormy sea, Jesus told the storm to subside, and it did! The terrified reaction of his fellow-travellers suggest that this wasn't just good timing on Jesus' part. They were prompted to ask each other, 'Who is this? Even the wind and the waves obey him!'[5]

Today, people question such accounts (we'll look at whether they're historically reliable in part 2), but at the time, no-one doubted that this impressive catalogue of miracles actually happened: even those who opposed him admitted as much.[6] They were the first to agree that Jesus had access to a supernatural, divine power.

> **No-one doubted that this impressive catalogue of miracles actually happened: even those who opposed him admitted as much.**

However, it is clear that Jesus thought himself to be more than just a man with *access* to a divine power; his words and actions frequently contained an implicit claim that he himself *is* that God. The religious 'experts' of the day (who didn't like Jesus' ministry) were among the first to realize this: on one occasion, they muttered, 'Why does this fellow talk like that? He's blaspheming! Who can forgive sins but God alone?'[7] They knew that Jesus was claiming to be God, and they could see that his extraordinary actions gave credence to his teaching.

Jesus' resurrection prompted people to worship him as God
If Jesus' life gives a strong indication that there is *someone* out there, and that *he* claimed to be God, it is his resurrection that substantiates his claim. Who can overcome death? No mere human can. Doctors can sometimes snatch someone back from the very edge of life and death, but if we met someone who'd been declared dead on a Friday afternoon, laid in a mortuary all of Saturday, and had then come back to life on the Sunday morning, the doctors would be freaked, and it would be difficult to treat that person as an ordinary human. But if there *is* a God who created life, then that God could overcome death as well. And if Jesus is that God in human form, we shouldn't be surprised that he rose from the grave.

> **If there is a God who created life, then that God could overcome death as well.**

It's instructive to look at people's reactions to Jesus after his resurrection. The two women who were the first to see him 'came to him, clasped his feet and worshipped him.'[8] Another of Jesus' close friends, Thomas, had a similar reaction – but only after he'd changed from being a hardened sceptic. For some reason, he hadn't been with Jesus' other friends when Jesus made one of his first resurrection appearances, and so when they later told him they'd seen Jesus alive again, he rubbished their claims, saying, 'Unless I see the nail marks in his hands and put my finger where the nails were, and put my hand into his side, I will not believe it.' A week later, he got his chance to do just that: Jesus appeared to the gathered group again, singled out Thomas and invited him to touch the scars from his execution. Jesus challenged him to 'Stop doubting and believe.' Able to touch Jesus physically, Thomas didn't need much convincing. His reaction was simple but profound – he simply called Jesus, this man he'd known for several years, 'My Lord and my God.'[9] He realized that Jesus' unique claims, made in life and apparently wiped out in death, had been gloriously confirmed in his resurrection.

It's important to realize that these were men and women who, although they firmly believed in God, did not expect God to pitch up in their midst, and wouldn't have dreamt of worshipping a fellow human. In fact, their whole belief system had to be completely reworked to make room for this assertion that Jesus was God. Understanding this background makes one former critic's bold attestations of Jesus' divinity all the more remarkable. Paul was initially convinced that Jesus was an evil man, but changed his mind having seen the resurrected Jesus for himself, and wrote that Jesus was 'declared with power to be the Son of God by his resurrection from the dead.' Elsewhere, he described Jesus as 'the image of the invisible God' and that God 'was pleased to have all his fullness dwell in him,' saying that Jesus was 'in very nature God.'[10]

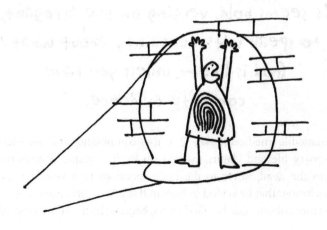

A few months ago, our house was burgled while we were out. The police came round later to look for fingerprints. Fingerprints aren't normally visible to the naked eye, so they scattered a fine powder in likely places, to see if a print would show up. Alas, none did in our case: the burglars presumably wore gloves. The police probably had a good idea of who committed the crime, but what they needed was evidence. You could say that the police were looking for the image of the (now) invisible burglars, but failed.

When Paul described Jesus as 'the image of the invisible God' it's as if he's saying, 'We've got a match! We know exactly what God looks like now, because we've got his fingerprint as evidence!'

The guessing games are over

That means that the days for speculation are over. It seems bold, verging on the arrogant, to speak with certainty about what God is like – unless you have concrete evidence. Jesus' life, death and resurrection give us that concrete evidence we need. If we just had Jesus' astonishing teaching and miracles to go by, we'd conclude that he was a great teacher and healer. If we just had his resurrection to go on, we'd imagine that he was the most

> It seems bold, verging on the arrogant, to speak with certainty about what God is like — unless you have concrete evidence.

remarkable medical fluke. But the combination of his extraordinary life and claims, backed up by his unique resurrection from the dead, never to die again, point us to a very different conclusion: that he is God in human flesh. We don't need to guess any more about whether God exists, because he has shown himself in Jesus. We don't need to guess any more about what God is like, because in Jesus, we can see exactly what he's like.

It's worth exploring God's character briefly, as we see it revealed in Jesus.

- On reading about Jesus' dealings with the sick and bereaved in his day, we discover that God is immensely caring: on many occasions, Jesus was 'deeply moved', 'filled with compassion', or wept when confronted with hurting people.[11]
- We find that God is interested in people no matter what their background or history. Jesus mixed with an extraordinary variety of people (prostitutes, farmers, tax-collectors and political leaders; party-goers and social recluses; Jews, Samaritans and Gentiles), and showed that he was willing to cross social, political, religious and racial boundaries.[12] And although Jesus saw thousands of people as he travelled, he would frequently pick out individuals – those who tried to hide in a crowd as well as those who hid from the crowd – and meet them at their point of need.[13]
- Jesus was particularly radical in his attitude towards women: in a society that viewed them as distinctly second-class, Jesus was not embarrassed to spend time with women and count them among his followers.[14]

In all this, it's clear from the vast crowds that followed Jesus wherever he went that he appealed to ordinary, everyday people. In fact, Jesus was very clear that his target audience wasn't the

Jesus appealed to ordinary, everyday people.

religious people, it was those who thought themselves beyond the scope of organized religion. I know of one church that advertises itself as 'A church for people who don't go to church': those are exactly the sort of people Jesus was, and is, after!

Is there anybody out there?

If the Christian claim that Jesus rose from the dead *is* true, then our searching for 'somebody out there' can stop, because we will have irrefutable evidence that there is a God. More than that, Jesus teaches us definitively, and shows us clearly, what God is like. We discover that God is wonderfully magnanimous and compassionate. Jesus taught that God created us, loves us, and wants each of us to know God personally, as our 'Father'. The introduction to John's biography of Jesus reflects on Jesus' coming into the world, and concludes, 'No-one has ever seen God, but God the One and Only [i.e., Jesus], who is at the Father's side, has made him known.'[15] The implication is clear: because God has revealed himself as a human person, we can get to know him.

However, if Jesus did *not* rise from the dead, we are no better off in our search for the Other – the something or someone which makes sense of those numinous moments. Jesus' contemporaries may have marvelled in his presence, but if he's now lying in a grave, he can't help us find answers to our questions.

real lives

Addlan comes from China and is doing a science doctorate at the University of Manchester.

Addlan, how do you know that God exists?

Growing up, I thought that matter and material things were all that existed: I didn't believe in any gods. I believed that things had positive and negative sides and harmony could only be achieved by mixing them properly. However, I felt that my life was lacking something so I started to learn ancient and modern philosophy and even tried to practise Buddhist meditation in order to understand the world around me. My mind was confused and my heart troubled. I needed peace desperately.

After arriving in the UK, I went to a café run by Christians to help international students settle down here, where I made some Christian friends. At first, I didn't believe that someone's life could change simply by accepting Jesus as their saviour. However, I found that Christians were nicer, more peaceful, and very friendly.

As a scientist, I am struck by the beauty of the universe, and think that it must be designed, not random. I learned from my new friends that the Bible says human beings were created by God in his own image, and that God has wisdom and God is love. The fact that there are laws and orders governing this universe and that love exists in human beings, makes me believe that there is a God.

Once I realized that God exists and God loves me, I studied the Bible more and decided to follow Jesus. I know that I have changed a lot. Before I was a Christian, I was envious, untrusting, judgmental, selfish, complicated and hopeless. But those attitudes were very destructive, hurtful and painful. I worried, I felt desperate, I was lonely and my heart had no rest. However, since I became a Christian, I have become simpler, and I feel released and healed.

real lives

Tammy is a research scientist and married Andrew in 2004. She lives in Stockport with their cat Treacle and loves running.

Tammy, why do you believe in God?

By the time I got to university, my priorities were career, sport and living life 'to the full' – God never came into the picture. Following a serious rugby injury, I found myself in hospital, very scared: What if I couldn't walk or play sport? What about my career? Then an authoritative yet loving voice resonated in my very bones. I knew it was God, asking me if I was paying attention. I could have died had the injury been 5 mm further up my spine; the next day, I walked out of hospital knowing I'd been granted a second chance.

Six months later, I went to church and instantly felt that I'd been called home. I met people who wanted to be my friends, helping me sort out my depression and alcoholism, as well as having a laugh together. They looked past my barriers and didn't judge me.

I realized that God wasn't out to spoil my fun, but that his 'rules' were there for my protection. I repented of my previous life, and the further I've travelled in my journey with him the more I've realized that going against him leads to pain and heartache.

Deep down inside, I know God exists. Some people say that science and Christian faith are incompatible but in my experience both work. Who told the bee how to produce such a mathematically precise honeycomb? Who gave the spider the ability to produce silk so strong that it's taken scientists years to emulate it? Sunsets look to us as if God has taken his art pallet and used the sky as his canvas. No mathematical equation can describe the awe and beauty of these wonders in nature. Exploring God's world scientifically advances technology but the ultimate answer came when God revealed himself in Jesus.

2. Why hasn't God done something about all the suffering?

We're so used to seeing the destruction caused by earthquakes, tsunamis, floods, hurricanes, famines and other disasters on television that we're in danger of becoming immune to the plight of countless millions of our neighbours in this global village. The twentieth century was one scarred by two world wars, and numerous other conflicts. The twenty-first century hasn't started any more peacefully. 'Genocide' is not a new evil, but is practised with increasing and disturbing regularity around the world. Almost every day another suicide bombing is reported, and world leaders are trying to fathom how best to conquer a new threat to world peace: international terrorism.

But even if our lives are untouched by disaster and unscathed by terrorism, our lives are seldom free from pain. Whenever our dreams are shattered into a thousand shards, or we find our nightmares being played out in slow-motion reality that is all too vivid, we bury our head in our hands and cry out, 'Why?' Trite answers from well-meaning friends only serve to exacerbate the pain.

Of course, if there is no God, then we cannot blame him for life's tragedies. We can only guess that suffering is a natural part of life, with little hope of it ending. But when Christians claim that there is a God, the problem of suffering becomes all the more pertinent: not just 'Why has this happened to me?' but 'Why has *God* let this happen to me?'

Even if our lives are untouched by disaster our lives are seldom free from pain.

After all, Christians say that God is both loving and all-powerful. If God is all-powerful, he should be *able* to do something to stop the suffering. If God is loving, he cannot *want* people to suffer. Therefore, if suffering happens, it is either because God is not all-powerful or because he is not loving. Even in the Bible, people shout at God with a sarcastic bitterness, 'Awake, O Lord! Why do you sleep? Rouse yourself! Do not reject us for ever. Why do you hide your face and forget our misery and oppression?'[1] Often there's an unspoken antagonism lurking in the background as well: it's all very well for God in heaven, where everything is perfect; but what does he know about suffering?

In a brief chapter like this, I cannot hope to give a comprehensive answer to these questions, still less to address individual situations you may be facing. My purpose rather, is quite limited: to show how Jesus' life, death and resurrection provide a key that begins to unlock new perspectives on the problems of suffering which can help us move forward in life with renewed confidence and hope.

Jesus suffered and can therefore comfort us
Merely to say that Jesus rose from the dead indicates that he first died, but his public execution was by no means his first experience

of suffering. One man predicted that Jesus would be 'a man of sorrows, and familiar with suffering',[2] and this description was painfully accurate. In a very conservative society, he had the social stigma of being born outside of wedlock. As a youngster, he was a refugee. As an adult, he was ridiculed by his family. It seems he was homeless for a while. His closest friends abandoned him when the going got tough. He knew the loneliness of not having a partner to share life with. He lived under an oppressive regime that reviled him. He mourned the loss of close friends, and probably his father as well. He was tried on false charges before a prejudiced court. He was tortured and then sentenced to one of the cruellest forms of death ever invented. If Jesus is God, then it is true to say that God himself has suffered and died. He knows what our pain-filled lives are like, and he hurts with us.

God is himself involved in the process of pain.

The suffering of innocent people seems unbearable if we imagine God as lounging in some celestial deckchair like a cosmic sadist, enjoying the sufferings of the world. But God is not indifferent to the pain of the world, and it is this caricature of God that was shattered at the cross. For there we see God, not on a deckchair but on a cross. He is himself involved in the process of pain.[3]

This Christian approach to suffering is radically different from the response of other religions. The poet Edward Shillito pointed this out powerfully. He fought in the First World War trenches, seeing more suffering than most twenty-first-century Western citizens have ever done, yet he wrote this about Jesus:

The other gods were strong, but Thou wast weak;
They rode, but Thou didst stumble to the throne;

But to our wounds, only God's wounds can speak;
And not a god has wounds, but Thou alone.[4]

One writer has drawn out this unique perspective on suffering particularly effectively, turning the question from 'How could God allow suffering?' to 'How could we believe in a God who doesn't suffer?' He writes:

I could never myself believe in God if it were not for the cross. . . . In the real world of pain, how could one worship a God who was immune to it? I have entered many Buddhist temples . . . and respectfully stood before the statue of Buddha, his legs crossed, arms folded, eyes closed, the ghost of a smile playing round his mouth . . . detached from the agonies of the world. But each time after a while I have had to turn away. And in my imagination I have turned instead to that lonely, twisted, tortured figure on the cross, nails through his hands and feet, back lacerated, limbs wrenched, brow bleeding from thorn-pricks, mouth dry and intolerably thirsty, plunged in God-forsaken darkness. That is the God for me! He laid aside his immunity to pain. He entered our world of flesh and blood, tears and death. He suffered for us.[5]

But why does God go to such lengths to suffer? One of the first Christian pastors explained that Jesus 'had to enter into every detail of human life' so that 'when he came before God . . . he would have already experienced it all himself – all the pain, all the testing – and would be able to help where help was needed.'[6] One of the early Christian leaders, Paul, testified to the reality of this comfort. He endured beatings, imprisonments, riots and shipwrecks, yet described God as 'The Father of compassion and the God of all comfort, who comforts us in all our troubles.'[7] Jesus suffered so that he can bring us comfort in our sufferings.

That's all very well. But does Jesus offer anything more than just a 'crutch for the weak'? What I've said so far still begs the question, 'Why hasn't God done something about all the suffering?'

Jesus' death and resurrection was a battle against evil

Suppose you go to see your local doctor with an internal chest pain. You'd probably be nervous as you explain your symptoms, fearful that something is up with your heart. The doctor listens through his stethoscope, smiles, and says, 'I think I know what the problem is.' He then launches into a long and complicated diagnosis of the problem, and explanation of why such a problem is giving you those particular symptoms. It's not long before he's lost you amidst all his technical terms. Feeling even more anxious now than you did before, you interrupt him, blurting out, 'Can you do anything about it? Is it curable?'

Intellectual explanations about suffering and pain are helpful only up to a certain point. When we're sitting in a wheelchair rather than an armchair, we'd rather have a solution. When Jesus died on the cross, God was doing more than empathizing with our suffering so that he could comfort us. He was beginning to deal with the very existence of evil and suffering, and our main adversary, death. He was beginning to work out his solution.

The Bible pictures Jesus' death as the turning-point in the war between God and evil. In a war, the 'winner' (if there ever is such a thing in war) is often the side that effectively disarms the opposition's worst weapon. For example, if one country's worst weapon is a missile, another country's anti-missile defence system is a key part of their campaign. Evil's worst weapon is death (which is why so many people are scared of death); so if Jesus were to conquer evil, he had to disarm death itself. The only way Jesus could disarm death was to meet it head-on, personally. That is what happened when he was executed: Jesus 'shared in [our] humanity

so that by his death he might destroy him who holds the power of death.'[8]

As Jesus died, it seemed as though death had triumphed. Yet the battle was not over. Jesus' resurrection is the vindication that Jesus fought, and won, the battle against evil on the cross. 'It was impossible for death to keep its hold on him,'[9] said one of Jesus' closest friends, Peter. If Jesus had remained in the grave, he would merely have been one more statistic of unjust suffering. But if, having died innocently, he was then raised from the dead, he has shown us that death, our ultimate enemy, is not invincible.

If we are on Jesus' side, we are on the winning side, for 'He suffered death, so that by the grace of God he might taste death for everyone.'[10] It was the assurance stemming from Jesus' triumph that enabled Paul to taunt the enemy, 'Where, O death, is your victory? Where, O death, is your sting?' and to proclaim that instead of death swallowing *us* up, '*Death* has been swallowed up in victory.' Rather than death *defeating* us, God 'gives us the *victory* through our Lord Jesus Christ.'[11]

Jesus' resurrection ushers in the new creation

But if Jesus has defeated death, why do people still die?

In any war, there is often a key battle after which the eventual outcome of the war is certain, but because of the pride or intransigence of the defeated side, they carry on fighting. Unwilling to admit defeat, the loser carries on trying to inflict damage on the victor. It takes a while before the inevitable outcome is confirmed.

The Bible pictures the war between God and evil as a cosmic war, on a cosmic timescale, which unfortunately means that although the key battle was won two thousand years ago in Jesus' death and resurrection, the war is still raging. The eventual outcome is certain (even though we don't know when it will be) – evil and death will be banished; peace will reign forever. Jesus' resurrection, then, doesn't just remind us to look for a glimmer of light in our darkest moments, it blinds us with the glorious and certain hope that a day will come when all suffering will stop, and that we can be part of that blissful reality. How does that work?

A day will come when all suffering will stop.

The Bible says that God created the world as a perfect place, and that one day, he will re-create that perfection in the 'new creation'. Our answer to the next question will spell out in more detail what this new creation will be like, but suffice it to say for now that it will have more in common with *this* world than with the Hollywood caricature of heaven's long-bearded inhabitants sitting on fluffy clouds looking comically resplendent in white nighties! In the vision of this new creation that Jesus gave to one of the church's early leaders, John, he records:

> I saw a new heaven and a new earth, for the first heaven and the first earth had passed away ... And I heard a loud voice from the throne saying, ' ... [God] will wipe every tear from their eyes. There will be no more death or mourning or crying or pain, for the old order of things has passed away.' He who was seated on the throne said, 'I am making everything new!' Then he said, 'Write this down, for these words are trustworthy and true.'[12]

It is clear that a significant way in which the new order will be different from our current one is that all suffering will have been eradicated. We're so used to stories of pain and suffering that we find it hard to imagine a world without any. But why not try, just for a moment? Imagine a world with no doctors, because everyone will be healthy; a place with no need for lawyers, because there'll be no arguments; a world without international tension or war, so no police or soldiers or peace-keeping forces. It's easy to work out what other jobs would cease to exist as well. But imagine also a world with no wheelchairs or Zimmer frames; no need for mouth braces, acne cream or pacemakers. If you've ever used any of those items, you'll know that you won't miss them one bit! Isn't it great to imagine a world like that?

In the Bible, Jesus' resurrection acts as the guarantee that this wonderful new creation will become a reality. Just as God breathed new life where there was death at Jesus' resurrection, so he will breathe new life into the whole of creation at the end of history. All traces of the stresses and strains that mar our current world will be blown away.

Some questions remain
I will never have all the answers to suffering, and I do not pretend that the three perspectives that I have given above answer all of my questions, let alone anyone else's. But I hope that together, Jesus' life, death and resurrection show that not only has God himself experienced human suffering, but also that he *has* done something about it, he *is* doing something about it, and he *will* do something about it.

In the death and resurrection of Jesus two thousand years ago, God did battle with, and defeated, our greatest enemy: death. Because of his suffering then, he is able to comfort us now. And one day, when the war is finally won, Jesus will usher in his new creation, devoid of all pain.

These Christian perspectives on suffering are quite unique, and give reassurance for the present and hope for the future. Evil will not have the last laugh.

But of course, if Jesus did *not* die and rise again, then such reassurance and hope is without foundation. We're left not only with our questions, but also our pain.

real lives

Darren is married to Karen. He works as an accountant and can't wait to take his twin toddlers to their first match at Manchester City Football Club.

Darren

Darren, how can you be a Christian when you've suffered so much?

I was born with cerebral palsy and the doctors told my parents I probably wouldn't live more than a few days, and if I did survive, I would never walk or talk. They were wrong!

When I was about three years old, my parents divorced. I grew up with my Dad (who remarried) but my step-brother bullied me. I also got bullied at school because of my disability.

I went to Sunday school every week, but church and God never really meant anything to me or had any effect on my life, until I was sixteen. I read the verse: 'The Lord does not look at the things man looks at. Man looks at the outward appearance, but the Lord looks at the heart.' It made me realize that I don't have to be anything special to be loved by God and that he loves me for who I am. So I decided to give my life to Jesus.

Despite being best friends with my Dad, I had to move out when he turned on me, so I ended up living with various Christian families from my church. But God has blessed me beyond all measure and I have been able to forgive my Dad, and we're now friends again. People often say to me, 'You've had a hard life and must feel really bitter', but I don't – and I put that down to God. Jesus never promised that Christians would be immune to suffering. Jesus himself suffered throughout his earthly life, which ended with death on a cross.

Life hasn't always been easy since becoming a Christian, but it's the best way to live! As a Christian, I believe and trust in a God who has suffered. God understands my suffering and he loves me unconditionally.

real lives

Slobodan fought in the Yugoslav army in the 1990s, and after meeting with Jesus Christ, studied at a Bible School in Serbia.

Slobodan, how can you believe in God when you've suffered so much?

I was a high-school dropout, and when I started working most of my money was spent on alcohol and cigarettes. After National Service, I got involved in gambling as well.

In 1991, civil war broke out. One night, at 3 am, the military police came to call me up. We were given uniforms and ammunition and were sent to a town in Croatia that was under a fierce attack. I saw my friends around me dying and losing body parts. That was the first time I started thinking about God. I said to him, 'If you exist, get me out of this hell in one piece.'

I came back in one piece, but not in good health. My life continued to go downhill. My mother was killed in a car accident; my father threw me out of the house; my brother was killed in a work accident. I became a squatter, lonely and completely unable to cope with my pain. I became very aggressive. My friends began to avoid me.

In 1999, NATO invaded our country and I cried out to God again. I tried committing suicide and was placed in a psychiatric hospital. I met a guy who was visited by young people who talked to him about Jesus. I met with them too and when I was discharged I attended my first church service. I felt warm inside and tears ran down my face. I prayed and became a Christian.

I've realized that I can't live in my own strength. When I go through difficult situations now, God helps me view them in a very different way. I don't get depressed or reach for false comforts any more. If Jesus had not given his life for me, I would still be living in ignorance, agony and darkness.

3. What happens when we die?

Death has been called the ultimate statistic: each one of us will die. One of the difficult privileges I have is meeting families when grief is raw, to prepare for the funeral of a loved one. When friends or family members die, we mourn because we've been robbed of their companionship. With time, the pain eases, but never goes away completely. In the months and years afterwards, even small things can trigger a fresh wave of grief.

But the death of people we love also makes us think about what will happen when *we* die.

A few years ago, I took part in a project which asked people their opinions on this subject. The answers were very varied. Some responded that they thought they would cease to exist: this life is all there is. On the face of it, this is the most plausible answer because, as the Humanist Manifesto puts it, 'There is no credible evidence that life survives the death of a body.'

Many responded that they believed in a heaven, but *not* a hell. Others were equally adamant that there was *both* a heaven *and* a hell. One thing was sure, of those who believed in a hell, very few imagined they would go there! The majority of us believe that as long as we try our best, and our good deeds outweigh our bad deeds, we will go to Heaven/Paradise/a better place. People are surprised to learn that this idea that heaven is a *reward* for a good life is more akin to the Muslim understanding of the afterlife than the Christian one.

Reincarnation is an increasingly popular idea, too. The 1990s film *Flatliners* and the more recent *What dreams may come* took this view when they portrayed the experience of life after death as being directly related to how we think and act in this world. Hinduism teaches that our rebirth depends on our karma. Many Buddhists also believe in reincarnation, with nirvana (nothingness) as the ultimate goal.

We'd love to know what happens when we die, but the difficulty is that with so many differing opinions and so few facts, any firm answers seem to be beyond our grasp.

> **If Jesus did rise from the dead, he is precisely the person to whom we should turn for answers.**

Our longing to find out what lies beyond the grave is not new. 'The Song of the Harper' is a four-thousand-year old Egyptian poem:

> No-one comes back from that place,
> To tell us how they live,
> To tell us what they need,
> To quieten our hearts until we go there.[1]

This poem hits the nail on the head: how can we know what lies beyond death unless someone comes back and tells us?

Of course, if Jesus *did* rise from the dead, he is precisely the person to whom we should turn for answers. Again, our guessing games (fun though they are) can stop, for we're suddenly presented with *evidence* rather than mere opinions. Crucially, if Jesus did rise from the dead, his resurrected body gives us clues as to what our bodies will be like after we die, and he is the one who can speak with authority about where we'll be.

Jesus' resurrection shows us what we'll be like after we die

As we read the accounts of Jesus' post-resurrection life, we find that Jesus had a recognizable physical body, which was partly similar to his pre-death body, and partly different. He could talk and eat like he did before, but he could also 'appear' and 'disappear', apparently at will. He still bore the wounds of his crucifixion, but they did not seem to hinder him. We'll examine these accounts in more detail in part 2.

For now, though, the important thing is to pick up the clues about what our own bodies will be like after we die. If we think about it, it's natural to assume that we'll all go through the same pattern of transformation, whatever that pattern may be. When daffodil bulbs are buried in the ground, it's not up to the individual bulb what happens to them, with some appearing as tulips, some as worms, some as daffodils and some as nothing! Rather, all daffodil bulbs, given the right conditions, emerge as daffodils. Similarly, what happens to us won't depend on what we *want* to happen to us, or what we *think* will happen. We'll all undergo the same process of transformation.

Thus, the clue from Jesus' transformed body is that we, too, will be resurrected. In the Bible, Paul says that 'in Christ [a title for Jesus], all will be made alive', and he describes Jesus as the 'first-fruits'[2] of those who have died, where a tree's 'first-fruits' were a guarantee of further fruit to come. In other words, Jesus' resurrection is a guarantee that *all* people will have a new life after death.

This then, is what our bodies will be like after we die: we will not cease to exist, nor will we be reincarnated as completely different beings, nor will we be disembodied spirits floating on clouds with halos and harps. Rather, we will have similar physical bodies to the ones we have at the moment, but with our existing ailments and imperfections eradicated.

If that gives us a strong clue about *what* our bodies will be like after death, what does Jesus say about *where* we will be?

Jesus' teaching tells us about the grim reality of hell

A popular view of Jesus is that he would not say 'boo' to a goose; in Christmas carols, we sing that he is 'gentle, meek and mild'. But his biographies record Jesus as saying some very harsh words, and giving some very uncomfortable teaching, not least on the subject of heaven and hell.

Jesus spoke frequently of hell as a real place, where some people would be banished. When talking with his friends about what would happen when they died, he told them, 'This is how it will be at the end of the age. The angels will come and separate the wicked from the righteous and throw them into the fiery furnace, where there will be weeping and gnashing of teeth.'[3]

Some people joke about wanting to go to hell, because 'At least my friends will be there.' Whether or not we take Jesus to be talking literally about a 'fiery furnace', one thing is clear: he is giving strong indications that no-one will find it enjoyable. There will be no friends in hell. In fact, it will be a place where all of God's good gifts that we enjoy in this life are notable for their absence.

That sort of place is almost as impossible for us to imagine as is the new creation, but C.S. Lewis tried to help us when he wrote *The Great Divorce*.

> I seemed to be standing in a bus queue by the side of a long, mean street. Evening was just closing in and it was raining. I had been wandering for hours in similar mean streets, always in the rain and always in evening twilight. Time seemed to have paused on that dismal moment when only a few shops have lit up and it is not yet dark enough for their windows to look cheering. And just as the evening never advanced to night, so my walking had never brought me to the better parts of town. However far I went, I found only dingy lodging houses ... I never met anyone. But for the little crowd at the bus stop, the whole town seemed to be empty. I think that was why I attached myself to the queue.

The others in his queue argue bitterly until a bus appears. Indeed, in the 'grey town', everyone continually quarrels with their neighbours, so there is a constant moving to the edge of town. As the town goes on expanding, it takes some people centuries just to get to the bus station. The inhabitants of the grey town live under the continual fear of the twilight turning into night.[4]

Lewis paints a thoroughly miserable and depressing picture, which helps us imagine what it would be like to be without such good things as trust, friendship, peace and beauty. Jesus implies that hell will be like that. I would not wish anyone – not even my worst enemy – to land up there.

Some people believe in purgatory as a temporary alternative to hell, from where everyone graduates to heaven having 'done their time' for any evil deeds committed in this life. As an idea, it's very appealing, especially after reading Jesus' teaching about hell!

However, Jesus never mentioned purgatory as a possible destination after death, and if he's the one person who's been through the grave and come back again, he's the only one who speaks with any authority or experience. He gave no indication of purgatory's existence, but every indication of hell's reality.

Jesus' teaching tells us about the wonderful reality of heaven

Fortunately, the answer to our question 'what happens when we die?', according to our 'been there, done that' tour-guide Jesus, is not all doom and gloom. Jesus also spoke of the 'kingdom of heaven' as being wonderful. 'The kingdom of heaven is like treasure hidden in a field,' he said. 'When a man found it, he hid it again, and then in his joy went and sold all he had and bought that field. Again, the kingdom of heaven is like a merchant looking for fine pearls. When he found one of great value, he went away and sold everything he had and bought it.'[5] Finding the kingdom of heaven is like finding the crown jewels – a priceless treasure. It is one of those moments in life that we will never forget.

What will heaven be like? Paul wrote that 'No eye has seen, no ear has heard, no mind has conceived what God has prepared for those who love him'.[6] It will be beyond our wildest imaginations. If we think of the most awesome view we've seen, the most intimate relationship we've shared, the deepest contentment we've felt, the most euphoric joy we've celebrated, or the most soul-inspiring experience we've enjoyed – and if we multiply that moment's intensity by infinity, and its duration by eternity, we'll have a glimpse of what it'll be like for the Christian to be with God in his new creation.

Some people imagine heaven to be intensely boring, involving floating in the air and listening to endless chanting, but the Bible characterizes the new creation as altogether more satisfying than that. The picture painted is one of tremendous community. John says, 'I looked and there before me was a great multitude that no-one could count, from every nation, tribe, people and language.'[7] This incredible cultural diversity won't have the associated problems of international rivalry and ethnic tension that we so often hear about and experience. In heaven, all peoples will be completely united around the risen Jesus. Heaven will also be a place of perfection, where no natural beauty is marred, no relationship suffers tension, and no pain exists. 'There will be no more death or mourning or crying or pain, for the old order of things has passed away.'[8]

> **Heaven will be a place of perfection, where no natural beauty is marred, no relationship suffers tension, and no pain exists.**

Most importantly, heaven is described as a place of deep friendship, not just with each other, but also with God. For the Christian, the crowning glory of heaven is that 'the dwelling of God is with men and women, and he will live with them. They will be his people, and God himself will be with them and be their God. He will wipe every tear from their eyes.'[9] To wipe someone's tear from their eyes is a beautifully intimate act, and encapsulates the closeness of the relationship that the Christian has with God. Paul's famous words sum up why the Christian longs for heaven: 'Now we see but a poor reflection as in a mirror; then we shall see face to face. Now I know in part; then I shall know fully, even as I am fully known.'[10]

As a Christian, I don't dread heaven as if it will be eternal drudgery. Rather, I eagerly anticipate it as I might excitedly look forward to seeing a friend whom I haven't seen in years, knowing that I'll have all the time in the world to spend enjoying their company. Heaven will be all that we long for this life to be: no suffering and no stress, in the company of the loving God who made us. I can't wait to get there!

Which is it to be: heaven or hell?

Crucially, Jesus said that what distinguished those who go to heaven and those who land up in hell was not how good or religious we are in this life, or how hard we try, but how we respond to Jesus and his claims.[11] We will look more closely at that in part 3. For now, the points to absorb are these: if Jesus did rise from the dead:

- Jesus' own resurrected body shows us that we will have similar bodies to our current ones after we die, yet without aches, pains or defects;
- Jesus speaks as an authoritative guide about where we will go when we die. As the one person who has come back from the dead, he is the only one who can tell us for definite what will happen when we die. He speaks of hell and heaven as equal and opposite realities: one worse than awful; the other better than glorious.

This is all very well, but slightly other-worldly! For many people, the question about what happens when we die isn't a philosophical one; it's a personal one they're forced to confront by the news that they have an incurable disease. Can Jesus' resurrection say anything to them?

Jesus' resurrection gives the Christian hope in the face of death

Our society avoids death whenever and wherever it can. Many people are afraid of dying and death, for it seems to be an entry into a great unknown. Woody Allen joked, 'It's not that I'm afraid to die; I just don't want to be there when it happens.'

Finding any hope in the face of death is nigh-on impossible, because death seems so final. However, if Jesus rose from the dead, then death is not the end, and we can have hope in the face of death. As the first generation of Christians were starting to die (some by martyrdom), Paul made it clear that his hope for the

future was grounded in Jesus' resurrection: 'Brothers and sisters, we do not want you to be ignorant about those who fall asleep [i.e. those who died], or to grieve like the rest of people who have no hope. We believe that Jesus died and rose again and so we believe that God will bring with Jesus those who have fallen asleep [died] in him.'[12]

It is an extraordinary thing to call death, that worst of enemies, by the name 'sleep', the best of friends! But if Jesus could raise people from death as easily as we can wake people from sleep, and if he himself conquered death and its power, then there is hope beyond the grave.

When one of Jesus' closest friends, Lazarus, had died and been in a tomb for four days, Jesus said to Lazarus' sister, Martha, 'I am the resurrection and the life. He who believes in me will live, even though he dies; and whoever lives and believes in me will never die.'[13] To prove his claim, Jesus proceeded to raise Lazarus from the dead. Later on, Lazarus was to die again, unlike Jesus. But Jesus had made his point: he has power over death, so that those who trust in him need not fear death. One early Christian preacher said that Jesus 'shared in our humanity so that by his death he might . . . free those who all their lives were held in slavery by their fear of death.'[14]

My grandfather once went to two funerals on the same day. One was a humanist funeral, and he described it as devoid of all hope. Death was the end, and the person leading the funeral could say nothing of solace or comfort in the face of death. If Jesus has not risen from the dead, we have no grounds for hope as we approach death.

The other funeral was that of a Christian, and my grandfather described it as an almost joyful event. Certainly, there was sadness, because those present had loved and would miss the dead man. But there was also gladness, because he had been relieved of his suffering, and had gone to be with his saviour and friend, Jesus Christ. All the Christians at that funeral knew that one day, they too would join him there. If Jesus did rise from the dead, we can have hope in the face of death.

real lives

Christine

Christine is forty-five years old, married with five daughters and two grandsons. Her own parents both died by the time she was thirteen. Eight months before writing this she was diagnosed with inoperable cancer and given six months to live.

Christine, how does being a Christian make a difference to you as you face death?

By my late twenties, I had three daughters and two divorces. Wanting my children to meet some stable families, I started going to my local church. People were very friendly and generous. It wasn't hard to go each week.

The minister prompted me to make a decision that he said would change my life. I didn't have anything to lose, so I did. No flashing lights, nothing remarkable at all. But everything began to change. I stopped drinking and flushed my anti-depressants away without suffering any physical reactions. I lost my totally irrational fear of dying at night. I was a million miles from the victim I'd let myself become.

My terminal cancer diagnosis came out of the blue. I didn't realize how much Jesus had made a difference until I heard a man get the same diagnosis as me. He was desperate. His family were silent apart from platitudes. What else could they say?

The diagnosis didn't hit me like that. Oh, it hurt like nothing else. I don't want to leave my family, my husband, my life. I've already passed my 'sell by date'. In Asda I'd be worthless now, but through the care and prayers of Christians, I feel more valued than I've ever felt. Cancer isn't the worst thing that's ever happened to me. With faith, it's possible to live with it.

Before the diagnosis I had hoped that the future in heaven was better then here. Now, inside, I have a certainty. I can't explain that, but my knowledge is built on experience and academic study. The first accounts in the Bible say witnesses 'saw' Jesus after he'd died. He proved it to lots of doubters. I know it holds true from past experience. I just wish I could convince more people to believe!

real lives

David

In 1983, David Watson, a prominent Christian leader and international speaker, was diagnosed with terminal cancer, and given a year to live. During that year, he wrote a book, 'Fear No Evil', charting the course of his disease and his ministry, from which these excerpts come.

The worst times for me were at two or three o'clock in the morning ... I had told countless thousands of people that I was not afraid of death since through Christ I had already received God's gift of eternal life. For years I had not doubted these truths at all. But now the most fundamental questions were nagging away ...

Did Christ really rise from the dead? I had for many years sifted through the evidence for this until I was sure beyond any reasonable doubt ... My confidence about the future was not just a psychological prop because I was frightened of death, nor was it clutching at some slender religious straw. Intellectually, I was as convinced as I possibly could be that Christ had risen from the dead, and this was the solid ground for my own future hopes. Death is not the end. Death is only putting out the lamp at the rise of a new dawn ...

When I die, it is my firm conviction that I shall be more alive than ever, experiencing the full reality of all that God has prepared for us in Christ ... The actual moment of death is still shrouded in mystery, but as I keep my eyes on Jesus I am not afraid. Jesus has already been through death for us, and will be with us when we walk through it ourselves.'

Shortly before David died, he said to a friend, 'I am completely at peace – there is nothing I want more than to go to heaven. I know how good it is.'[15]

4. Does life have a meaning or purpose?

Few people are prepared to admit that their lives are mere accidents. One Buddhist professor said that, 'The chances that life just occurred on earth are about as unlikely as a typhoon blowing through a junkyard and constructing a Boeing 747.' That leaves each of us with a nagging question in our minds. As Madonna put it, 'I'm sure everyone's had that out-of-body experience where you say to yourself . . . why am I here?'[1] One columnist highlighted the urgency of the question: 'Why do I *have* to know why I was born? Because, of course, I am unable to believe that it was an accident; and if it wasn't one, it must have a meaning.'[2]

Some people try to find a meaning in life by being good to those around them. Others have told me, very nobly, that their aim in life is to provide a better world for their children, and this gives them a sense of purpose and meaning.

Douglas Coupland is an author who has put his finger on the restlessness that many in our generation feel. *Girlfriend in a Coma* follows the lives of four Vancouverites as they look for meaning in life. One day, one of the four, Linus, suddenly ups and leaves, and spent the next few years 'gadabouting' around the States, doing odd jobs when necessary. In a postcard back home, Linus explains his actions:

You asked why I'm doing this and that's a reasonable question. I think I couldn't see my hitting into the everyday world any longer. I found myself doing electrical work day in/day out and realised I would have to do this the rest of my life and it spooked me. I don't know if there's some alternative out there, but I spend most of my time wondering what it might be. I suppose there's always crime, but that's not good when you're older. There's drugs, but you know, I've never seen anybody who's been improved by drugs. Life seems both too long and too short. This being said, I had a good day today. The clouds were pretty and I bought a sack of clothes at the goodwill store for five bucks.

Later on in the story, while other characters 'still believe that meaning could pop into [their lives] at any moment', Linus gives his conclusion on life:

You know, from what I've seen, at 20 you know you're not going to be a rock star. By 25, you know you're not going to be a dentist or a professional. And by 30, a darkness starts moving in – you wonder whether you're ever going to be fulfilled, let alone wealthy or successful. By 35, you know, basically, what you're going to be doing the rest of your life; you become resigned to your fate.[3]

Such bleak pessimism haunts many. Prince Charles has said, 'There remains deep in the soul, if I may use that word, a persistent and unconscious anxiety that something is missing; some ingredient that makes life worth living.'[4] The columnist quoted earlier describes this anxiety as an 'ache':

Countries like ours are full of people who have all the material comforts they desire, together with such non-material blessings as a happy family, and yet lead lives of quiet, and at times noisy, desperation, understanding nothing but the fact that there is a hole inside them and that however much food and drink they pour into it, however many motor cars and television sets they stuff it with, however many well balanced children and loyal friends they parade around the edges of it ... it aches.'[5]

Many people try to ignore this ache by filling their lives with busyness, as if meaning could be found by sheer levels of activity. Bob Geldof, who raised £50m for LiveAid and staged Live8 to highlight the ongoing concerns of many about African poverty, showed a disarming honesty in one interview when he admitted, 'I am unfulfilled as a human being.' Thumping his chest, he continued:

> Everything I do is because I'm frightened of being bored, because
> I know that's what's down in these holes. I'm frightened of it;
> it makes me very depressed. So I stay active. Frenetically so,
> unfortunately. And that freneticism keeps me going all the time
> and allows me to think I'm not wasting my time.[6]

Others resign themselves to the conclusion that there is no meaning in life, and so decide to live for themselves, for the moment. They play hard and fast. Their motto is 'Eat, drink and be merry, for tomorrow we die.'[7]

But is it true that there is no meaning or purpose in life? Do we have to dull the ache of our restless searching with either busyness or hedonistic living? Or could Jesus' life, death and resurrection provide clear direction to our meandering path through life?

Jesus' resurrection tells us that this life's meaning is found only in the light of eternity

Jesus made the incredible claim, 'I have come that [those who follow me] may have life, and have it to the full.'[8] Far from draining all the juice from life, being a follower of Jesus is the way to finding true life, including true meaning in life. How?

Jesus repeatedly warned his listeners against finding meaning in the material things of this life. 'Watch out!' he said. 'Be on your guard against all kinds of greed; a person's life does not consist in the abundance of their possessions.' He followed this up with a story of a rich businessman whose fortune kept growing, to the extent that he planned to tear down his current warehouses in order to build bigger ones to store all his assets. 'You have plenty of good things laid up for many years,' the businessman said to himself. 'Take life easy; eat, drink and be merry.' Jesus says that God's response in that situation was very sharp: 'You fool! This very night your life will be demanded from you. Then who will get what you have prepared for yourself?' Jesus spelt out the conclusion, 'This is how it will be with anyone who stores up things for themselves but is not rich towards God.'[9]

We all know that we cannot take anything with us when we die, and yet many of us still look to money and material possessions to provide meaning and happiness. And this despite many of the rich and famous telling us that they have found little happiness in their wealth. Australian comedian Barry Humphreys, who plays the cult figure Dame Edna Everage, begins his autobiography,

I always wanted more. I never had enough milk or money or socks or sex or holidays or first editions or solitude or gramophone records or real friends or guiltless pleasure or neck-ties or applause or unquestioning love. Of course, I've had more than my fair share of most of these commodities but it always left me with a vague feeling of unfulfilment. Where was the rest?[10]

Kenneth Williams, the hugely successful British actor, simply wrote in his diary, 'I wonder if anyone will ever know the emptiness of my life?' Boris Becker, the former tennis star, came close to taking his own life through being overwhelmed by a sense of hopelessness and lack of meaning. He said,

> I had won Wimbledon twice before, once as the youngest player. I was rich. I had all the material possessions I needed; cars, women, everything ... I know that this is a cliché: it's the old song of the movie and pop stars who commit suicide. They have everything and yet they are so unhappy ... I had no inner peace. I was a puppet on a string.[11]

Jesus says that true satisfaction comes not through amassing material possessions in this life, as if this life is all there is to live for, but in understanding our lives from an eternal perspective. Jesus' resurrection shows us that there *is* life beyond the grave, and that there is a spiritual dimension to our lives. There is an alternative to living for the moment: living for eternity, storing up 'treasures in heaven'. Whereas material possessions need constant attention and protection, 'treasures in heaven' are guaranteed, because 'no thief comes near and no moth destroys'.[12] There is an alternative to our frequently selfish lives: living for God, being 'rich towards God'. Jesus promised that to those who 'seek first [God's] kingdom and his righteousness, all these [material] things will be given to you as well.'[13]

The apostle Paul put Jesus' words into practice, and discovered that it was 'the secret of being content in any and every situation, whether well fed or hungry, whether living in plenty or in want.'[14] That is the declaration of someone who has found meaning in life – by looking at their life in the context of eternity.

Jesus' resurrection tells us that we can find meaning through a friendship with God

There is a saying in psychology that a person does not know

who they are until they know *whose* they are. In other words, our closest relationships help to provide our identity. Our human experience is that relationships can give the highest joy in life, so it's natural that many find purpose and meaning through their closest relationships. But where a relationship is broken or lacking, we also experience the deepest heartache. Freddie Mercury, one of the greatest pop stars ever, blamed his extreme loneliness on his success.

> You can have everything in the world and still be the loneliest man, and that is the most bitter type of loneliness. Success has brought me world idolisation and millions of pounds, but it's prevented me from having the one thing we all need – a loving, ongoing relationship.[15]

His tragic sadness is repeated in millions of hearts around the world. We long for a 'loving, ongoing relationship', but such relationships seem to be becoming ever more elusive.

It is not surprising that the second part of Jesus' answer to our quest for meaning and purpose in life is to point us to a relationship, and one which is 'loving and ongoing'. What may be surprising is that just such a friendship is possible with God, the one who made us, through Jesus, the one who died yet is alive again.

A Christian is someone who *knows* God – not just as an intellectual concept, but as a friend. In the Bible, Abraham was described as God's friend.[16] Jesus' own definition of 'eternal life' was 'that [people] may *know* the only true God, and Jesus Christ whom [God] has sent.'[17] Jesus taught his followers to call God their 'Father', indicating that they could have a very intimate relationship with God.[18] Years after Jesus' death and resurrection, the apostle Paul talked of the 'surpassing greatness of *knowing* Christ Jesus my Lord, for whose sake I have lost all things.'[19] When Christians pray, they are not talking to thin air or a brick wall; they are talking to the living Jesus who can hear and answer our prayers.

Those who know God vouch that his love is unwavering. God describes himself as 'the compassionate and gracious God, slow to anger, abounding in love and faithfulness, maintaining love to thousands, and forgiving wickedness.'[20] That is a stunning and beautifully tender claim that many of God's friends in the Bible and Christians since can verify. God's love is also unconditional: even when Christians let God down, he still sticks by them. Jesus described God's love for us as like a Father on the lookout for his wayward son, who had spurned his love and run away from home. 'While [the son] was still a long way off, his father saw him and was filled with compassion for him; he ran to his son, threw his arms around him and kissed him. . . . The father said, "Let's have a feast and celebrate." '[21] What better 'loving, ongoing relationship' could we want?

Jesus' coming back to life, never to die again, means that he is alive today, and that we can know him, even though we cannot see him. Jesus says that our deepest longings are satisfied – not in searching for wealth or fame, nor in living for the moment, nor even in strong human relationships – the deepest satisfaction comes through knowing our maker. It is only he who can make us truly ourselves. We do not know who we are until we have worked out whose we are.

Our human hearts were made by God, for God, and our hearts' restlessness will cease only when we begin a friendship with God. Maybe our restlessness is like a 'homing instinct'. Swallows and other migrant birds confidently fly to countries thousands of miles away. Salmon return to spawn in the rivers of their birth. Although we often do not realize it, we have something like a 'homing instinct' which is trying to take us back to our maker.[22] For some people, that process takes years. Many, tragically, suppress their homing instincts, and never find their way 'home'.

Augustine was a thinker who searched restlessly for years to find meaning and purpose. After he became a Christian, he prayed to God, 'You have made us for yourself, and our heart is restless until it rests in you.'[23] I remember visiting a lady who'd been twice bereaved. She said to me, 'I feel like I've got this hole inside, and I just can't fill it.' A few weeks later, she became a Christian, and her life changed dramatically. The pain of human loss was still there, but she knew that a deeper emptiness had been filled.

Does life have a meaning or purpose?

Jesus said that he came to give life in all its fullness, and the experience of millions of Christians is that he does just that, giving a meaning and purpose to life that satisfies their deepest longings. Jesus' resurrection alerts us to the fact that there is more to this life than the few years we live on Planet Earth; our meaning comes through looking at our lives from the perspective of eternal life. Jesus said, 'I am the bread of life. Whoever comes to me will never go hungry, and whoever believes in me will never be thirsty.'[24] Jesus' resurrection also means that we can have a real friendship with the God who made us – the ultimate 'loving, ongoing relationship'.

Of course, if Jesus did not rise from the dead, we are thrown back into the bleak reality of searching desperately for meaning in life where there is none; still hunting for that elusive perfect relationship.

real lives

Laura works in Khayelitsha, a shanty town which is home to 1½ million people on the outskirts of Cape Town, South Africa.

Laura, what difference has being a Christian made to you?

At sixteen, I left my convent school and quickly learned how to smoke, drink, and go out with loads of men. I soon became the life of the party. At twenty-two, I decided to make my fortune. I had all I thought I needed to be happy: a new car, loads of friends, a trendy place to live, the best clothes, expensive drinks. I went to parties and clubs almost every night. But I had no inner peace.

I married the man I had been living with, but instead of fulfilment, I found unhappiness. He was jealous, quick-tempered and abusive. One day he vanished, leaving me with his huge debt. My world collapsed. All my self-confidence, independence, and self-sufficiency were gone. I ended up in a psychiatric ward, then a home for drunks.

Soon after, a friend's life was radically changed. Her incessant swearing stopped, and she started going to church. Intrigued by what she said about her church, I went along. The church was packed, and the minister spoke of a solution to my wicked ways. I was mortified, but because I wanted God to change my life, I prayed his prayer. I thought I'd be an instant angel, but instead, I got worse. It took me several weeks to realize that God had taken up residence in me, and now I needed to let him change me.

It was wonderful! All my sin and wicked ways were forgiven and forgotten. The hurt and pain went. I finally had peace, contentment and fulfilment. God healed me of drinking and drugs, and these past twenty-eight years I have served Him. It's a pleasure to be alive, in spite the problems of daily living. God helps me cope with anything.

Laura's work in Khayelitsha started with a makeshift pre-school nursery for a few children roaming the streets. Her work now reaches hundreds of families, offering professional pre-school facilities, sponsorship for schooling and skills-teaching for parents. Alongside this, Laura has helped establish various Bible study groups, Sunday schools and churches.

real lives

Slava

Slava is a waiter in Russia, studying to become a film director.

Slava, what difference has being a Christian made to you?

Before I met Jesus, I was filled with cynicism, and an all-consuming desire to get noticed. I made lots of jokes, usually to prove others ridiculous and myself smart. I had been passionate about all kinds of achievements hoping to find happiness in that. I desperately wanted people to depend on me and love me, so I strived to earn money, to become the best in mathematics, to buy beer for friends . . . But all this didn't work and pain and loneliness wouldn't leave me.

I came to know Christ through meeting a man at my local church who could loan me money. I hated worship songs and despised all the Christians, but soon I heard about Jesus and his death, which could prevent me going to hell. I had no choice but to come to Christ and offer him my life. I thank God that he loved me so much and knew me so well that he found a way to my heart.

Knowing Christ has made all the difference. In him I've found a love I couldn't dream of. But I also realized that I was no different from others: the bad things they would do to me, I would do myself. But Christ has made me different. Having felt his love, he's been teaching me how to love others. I've learned to respect people and to appreciate what they have inside more than outside. I've discovered the freedom to be myself, and to make mistakes. And relationships matter a whole lot now because I know I don't have to be afraid of them. They're risks worth taking. My life with Christ is worth living.

5. Which religion, if any, is true?

Within a couple of miles of my home, I can walk to several Muslim mosques, a Sikh temple, a Baha'i information centre, a variety of different Christian churches ('high' church, 'low' church, Catholic, Church of God of Prophecy, Church of England, Methodist, Baptist, independent, Salvation Army, Seventh Day Adventist), a sect or two and a Jewish synagogue. When I catch the bus, I see posters advertising meditation according to Buddhist principles. When I stroll through the park, I occasionally see people practising a form of yoga. If I wander into a bookshop, the 'religion and spirituality' section includes books on half a dozen other spiritual ideas that I have never even heard of. To someone with no experience of religion, the choice is bewildering. How can they know where to start? How could any religion possibly make an exclusive claim to be 'true' when there are so many alternatives?

It is very common for those with little religious adherence to suppose that all religions lead to God: there is one great (probably unknowable) God, and the claims of different religions are just reflections of different aspects of that same God. Accordingly,

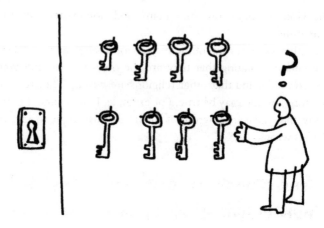

none of the religions should claim definitive knowledge about God, although they can contribute to the sum of our knowledge about he/she/it.

It is an attractive idea, and if everyone accepted it, the various atrocities committed under the name of religious fundamentalism might stop. However, there are two basic problems with this view. The first is that to say 'All religions lead to God' is in itself a claim to a definitive knowledge about God and religions. In claiming such definitive knowledge, it is doing precisely what it tells others to avoid! In the process, it actually becomes a supremely arrogant claim, although most people don't realize that. It is also a claim with very weak foundations, based not on evidence, but on little more than wishful thinking.

The second problem is that ordinary believers in some of today's world religions realize that there are irreconcilable differences between their varied understandings of 'God'. For example, a Buddhist's claim that the ultimate reality is a void, an emptiness, cannot be reconciled with a Jew's claim that God is a personal being. A Muslim's claim that there is only one God is incompatible with the Shinto believer's claim that there are many Gods. It takes some very obscure reasoning to suggest that these varied understandings of the nature of God could actually all be true. God cannot be 'one' and 'many' and 'non-existent' all at the same time!

Furthermore, several of the major world religions make claims to exclusivity, stating that they are the only way to understand God correctly, and that other religions are wrong. They're either all wrong, or one may be true. For example, Islam cannot be right to say that Judaism is wrong if Judaism is also right to say that Islam is wrong.

> **God cannot be 'one' and 'many' and 'non-existent' all at the same time!**

So although it would be nice to suppose that all religions are equal, or at least, partial contributors to our overall knowledge of God, given the inherent flaws with this view, that cannot be so. How, then, can we ascertain which of the competing religious claims, if any, are true? Can Jesus' life, death and resurrection speak with clarity through the cacophony of competing answers? I want to suggest that Jesus is unique among the founders of world religions, and that the Christian accounts of his death and resurrection are far more reliable, historically speaking, than other accounts. If these points are true, Jesus' claim to be the only way to God is given great weight, and should be the starting point of any serious spiritual enquiry.

Jesus' life and death are unique among religious leaders

Moses died, according to Jewish tradition, at the age of one hundred and twenty. They say his eyes were undimmed and his vigour unfaded. He was the hero of the Jewish nation.

Buddha died at the age of eighty, in peaceful serenity, as you might expect. He was surrounded by a great host of devotees, whom he had won to his philosophy.

Confucius died at the age of seventy-two. He had returned to his home of Lu in triumph over his opponents; he had successfully organized a large company of noble disciples to continue his work.

Muhammad died at the age of sixty-two, having thoroughly enjoyed the last years of his life as political ruler of a united Arabia. He passed away in his harem at Mecca, in the arms of his favourite wife.

Christianity's founder has a strikingly different story.

Some people claim that the origin of all religions is basically the same: that they are the creation of men of great personal devotion who uncover some basic human truths and devote their lives to teach those truths, perhaps forming a culture or sub-culture around them. As far as Judaism or Buddhism or Confucianism or Islam go, there is credibility in that opinion. Their leaders all died in ripe old age, after a lifetime of teaching, in the midst of vast popular acclaim, with the future of their movements guaranteed.

Christianity's founder has a strikingly different story. Jesus died somewhere around the age of thirty-three, after a teaching ministry of, at the very most, three years. He was ostracized by his society. He had been betrayed and denied by his own supporters. He had been mocked by his opponents. He had been forsaken by everyone, even, he said as he was dying, by God himself. He suffered one of the most brutal and humiliating forms of public execution ever devised by the cruel imagination of humanity. His followers scattered, and the future of his movement appeared doomed. The contrast between Jesus and the founders of other world religions could hardly be greater.[1]

Another huge difference is that while members of some other world religions *commemorate* the death of their founder, Christians actually *celebrate* Jesus' death, and do so regularly. In a later chapter, we will see that this is because Christians recognize Jesus' death as the climax of his mission, rather than a tragic end to his life. The apostle Paul even wrote, 'May I never boast except in the cross of our Lord Jesus Christ.'[2] Both Jesus' life and death are unique among religious leaders.

While members of some other world religions commemorate the death of their founder, Christians actually celebrate Jesus' death.

When it comes to Jesus' death and resurrection, at least two of the major religions are wrong

In part 2 of this book, we will examine closely the historical evidence surrounding Jesus' death and resurrection. This section will simply look at the differing claims that the three great historically-based religions (Judaism, Islam and Christianity) make about those events.

As the *Jewish* scriptures date from before Jesus, they have no record of his life, but the traditional Jewish understanding is that Jesus died on the cross, and remained dead. He was a blasphemer worthy of the death penalty, and certainly not the Messiah. To a Jewish person, it is an abhorrent thought that the Messiah would die on a cross. Christianity sprang from Judaism, with many of the early Christians from Jewish backgrounds. Within a few decades, the religions had split over the crucial issue of Jesus' death and resurrection, and the Jewish authorities vehemently tried to stop the Christians from spreading their message.

The *Islamic* scriptures (the Qur'an) were written hundreds of years after Jesus' death. He is mentioned several times, and is even called the Messiah. Muslims honour Jesus as a prophet, and like Christians, believe that Jesus was born of the virgin Mary and will come back one day. However, when it comes to the events surrounding Jesus' death, direct contradiction emerges. Surah 4.157 in the Qur'an, speaking of Jesus' death, states that: 'They did not kill him and they did not crucify him, but it appeared so to them . . . they did not kill him for certain.' Rather than being killed, 'Allah took him [Jesus] up to Himself' (Surah 4.158). Some Muslims believe that it was *not* Jesus upon the cross, but someone else (maybe Judas) who looked like Jesus. Other Muslims believe that it *was* Jesus on the cross, but that he did not die; it merely looked as if he died, whereas in fact Allah had taken him directly to himself.

In contrast to Jews and Muslims, *Christians* believe that it was Jesus who died on the cross, and that he did come back to life, never again to die.

It should be obvious that these three differing versions of the events of that first Easter cannot all be true. Either one is true, or none are true. If the Jewish or Muslim claims could be verified – that Jesus did not die at all, or that he did die but did not rise again – then the Christian faith would collapse. It's vital that we get to the truth on this crucial historical question – but how?

> **Christians believe that it was Jesus who died on the cross, and that he did come back to life, never again to die.**

In any historical investigation, the most reliable information is that written closest to the events under examination. For example, to learn about the Norman Conquest of Britain (1066), British children study the Bayeux Tapestry, which was made shortly after. And when learning about the Great Fire of London (1666), they read Samuel Pepys' diary, written at that time. If someone were to come up with new theories about those events now, but not produce any supporting evidence from closer to the time, their theories would be quickly dismissed.

So, when it comes to examining the competing claims about Jesus' death and resurrection, which are the earliest – and therefore most reliable – documents? The Qur'an was penned by one man, nearly six hundred years after Jesus' death and resurrection, and there is no external written supporting evidence for its claims. By contrast, most of the Bible's varied accounts of Jesus' death and resurrection were written forty to fifty years after the initial events; some much earlier. There is further external supporting evidence within seventy years of the events.[3]

In light of these dates, no academic historian would give the Qur'anic accounts much credence in comparison to the accounts written over five hundred years earlier – and very close in time to the original events being described. Readers must make up their own minds which account they will accept as most likely to be true.

Jesus' resurrection and its implications are unique among world religions

Muhammad's body is buried at Medina, and his tomb is visited by tens of thousands of people every year. Nobody claims that he rose from the dead. The Buddha's body was cremated, and his ashes distributed among eight groups of his followers. Nobody claims that he rose from the dead. Moses was buried in Moab, but the location of his grave is unknown. Nobody claims that he rose from the dead.

Christianity is quite unique in claiming that its historical founder rose from the dead. Nobody could produce the body as proof that he was still dead, even though his corpse was supposedly under Roman guard after his crucifixion.

It did not take long for Jesus' followers to realize that his resurrection had immense significance. An early Christian statement of faith said that Jesus 'was declared with power to be the Son of God, by his resurrection from the dead.'[4] Such incredible claims that Jesus was God, had become a human, and was alone worthy of worship were just as contentious then as they are now, for Middle-Eastern society was just as multi-cultural and multi-religious two thousand years ago as it is today. The main cities were peppered with temples to different gods, and the Roman emperor demanded total worship and allegiance.

C.S. Lewis helped to draw out the magnitude of the Christian claim that its human founder was actually God himself. He wrote:

> If you had gone to Buddha and asked him, 'Are you the son of Bramah?' he would have said 'My son, you are still in the vale of illusion.'
>
> If you had gone to Socrates and asked 'Are you the son of Zeus?' he would have laughed at you.
>
> If you had gone to Mohammed and asked 'Are you Allah?' he would first have rent his clothes and then cut your head off.
>
> If you had asked Confucius 'Are you heaven?' he would probably have replied, 'Remarks which are not in accordance with nature are in bad taste.'[5]

By contrast, when Jesus was on trial, the high priest said to him, 'I charge you under oath by the living God: Tell us if you are the Christ, the Son of God.' (To be 'the Christ' and 'the Son of God' pretty much amounted to being God.) Jesus replied, 'Yes, it is as you say.'[6]

Which religion, if any, is true?

Jesus stands out as unique among the great religious leaders the world has seen. No other religion claims that the death of its founder is central to its message. No other religion claims that its founder rose from the dead. No other religion claims that its founder was uniquely divine. No other religion can produce the dramatic evidence for the existence and character of God that Jesus did by his resurrection.

If Jesus did not rise from the dead, he is not unique, and he can be relegated to one idea among many. But if he did rise from the dead, we must take his claim to be God with the utmost seriousness. Furthermore, when trying to ascertain which (if any) of the religions are true, it makes sense to start by assessing the Christian claim that Jesus rose from the dead. If he did, we immediately have our answer about other religions; if he didn't, we can dismiss Christianity from our search for the truth. As one writer put it:

> If Jesus did rise from the dead, then he is indeed the way to God. God has vindicated him and set him on high. In that case the exclusiveness of the Christian claim makes sense. It does not amalgamate with other faiths, because it is so very different. The risen Jesus is not just one of the many, he is unique. It is not that Christians are narrow-minded or uncharitable about other faiths. But if Jesus is indeed, as the resurrection asserts, God himself who has come to our rescue, then to reject him, or even to neglect him, is sheer folly. That is why Jesus is not, never has been, and never can be, just one among the religious leaders of mankind. He is not even the best. He is the only. Among various examples of the relative he stands out as the absolute. In the risen Jesus, God Almighty confronts us with shattering directness. . . . If we conclude that Jesus Christ did indeed rise from the dead, then that settles the question of other religions.[7]

Let the investigation begin!
Throughout part 1, we've found that the life, death and resurrection of Jesus is a key which begins to unlock some answers to life's big questions. That makes it all the more important to determine what actually happened that first Easter. If the Christian claims about Jesus are true, we have met God himself in the person of Jesus, and we have started to find answers to life's biggest questions. If the Christian claims are shown to be false, the answers that I've given in these chapters are also false. It's time for our detailed investigation to begin.

real lives

Abdullah, a Malay, lives in a rural Muslim village in South East Asia. He is now getting on in years, but used to work as a rubber tapper. He is married and has six children.

Abdullah

Abdullah, what made you leave Islam and follow Jesus?

My friend Yusuf was a convicted criminal and spent ten years of his life behind bars. But on his release from prison he was a different man. His life had completely changed. He was friendly and polite. His relationship with his wife improved. He became a helpful and cheerful person.

One day, I asked him what had caused such a change. He replied by asking me, 'Where is Isa al-Masih at present?' (Isa al-Masih is the Muslim title for Jesus Christ. Muslims believe that Isa – Jesus – was a prophet of God, and that he is presently alive with God in heaven, having been rescued from earth before crucifixion.)

I answered, 'Isa is in heaven with God!'

Yusuf asked me a second question, 'And where is Muhammad, the prophet of Islam, at present?'

'The prophet lies dead in his grave,' I answered.

Yusuf smiled and then he asked me, 'So, Abdullah! Who do you want to follow? A dead prophet or a living one?'

I was speechless, I stood there with my mouth open, but could not say a word. I had never thought about this matter before (I was happy as I was), but somehow I knew that this was the most important question of my life.

Yusuf's words would not leave me alone. Muhammad is dead. Jesus Christ is alive. If Jesus lives and is coming back again, then he must be almighty. If he is really alive, then I must put my faith in him. I could do nothing else but follow him.

I wanted to find out more, so I saw Yusuf again the next day and together we visited some Christian friends of his. They explained many things about Jesus to me. Then we prayed together and I committed my life to Isa al-Masih – Jesus Christ.

Names have been changed to protect identities. Yusuf was later killed, for being a Christian.

real lives

Somchai, who was once a Buddhist priest, now pastors a church in Bangkok.

Somchai, what made you leave Buddhism and follow Jesus?

When I first became a Buddhist priest, I was very conscientious. But as I started to observe those who had been in the priesthood for some time, I became puzzled, then disillusioned.

At first, I thought Christianity was a foreigner's religion and dismissed it. But I got a Bible and read it from start to finish in two months. I felt I needed to look at these two very different faiths and make a decision.

When I finally accepted Jesus, I immediately experienced an immense peace, as well as the assurance that I was going to heaven, that I had escaped my *karma*, and didn't have to bear the consequences of the cycle of *karma*. God knows us personally and is the one who can change us.

As we turn to God there is always a response on his part. We all need answers to life. I went looking for these answers, and I found Jesus Christ. I was once a Buddhist monk, now I'm a Christian pastor in Thailand.

part two

Is it true?

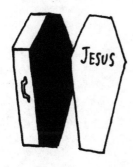

Investigating the evidence around
Jesus' resurrection

part two

Is it true?

6. Looking at the evidence

In part 1, I asked you to *suppose* that Jesus rose from the dead. That was so that we could work out whether or not Jesus' resurrection was going to be relevant to us. I hope you'll agree by now that, if true, Jesus' resurrection does indeed begin to open up some answers to the big questions we all ask.

In part 2, I don't want you to *suppose* that Jesus came back from the grave – far from it! I'm inviting you to *investigate* (with as many brain cells as you can muster) the evidence surrounding that remarkable claim. The question is: is it true or not? Did Jesus rise from the dead?

I don't want to make any assumptions about how much you already know about the supposed events of Jesus' death and the weeks following, so in this chapter, I'll present the evidence as we've received it down the centuries. Chapter 7 will, in effect, cross-examine the witnesses, to gauge whether or not the evidence presented is reliable. Only then, in chapters 8 and 9 can we seriously investigate the competing theories of what really happened to Jesus.

It's time to put your thinking caps on . . .

Evidence from non-Christian sources

Besides all the records in the Bible, there are several ancient historians who describe Jesus' life, and many other early religious writings that speak about Jesus. Together, they provide such overwhelming evidence for the existence of a man called Jesus that no serious academic doubts as much. But what was his life like? We'll start by looking at the accounts found outside the Bible, written by those who weren't Christians.

The most famous Jewish first-century historian was called Josephus. He wrote:

> About this time arose Jesus, a wise man, if indeed one ought to call him a man. For he was one who wrought surprising feats and was a teacher of such people who accept the truth gladly. He won over many Jews and many of the Greeks.[1]

Josephus clearly alludes to Jesus' miracles and the cross-cultural appeal of his teaching. Associating Jesus with wisdom and truth, he even acknowledges that he was no normal human. But what about Jesus' death?

Again, very few credible historians doubt that Jesus really did die, because contemporary ancient historians mention his execution. Josephus describes how, 'Pilate, upon hearing [Jesus] accused by men of the highest standing amongst us, ... condemned him to be crucified.'[2] Tacitus, the greatest of Roman historians of the period confirms that

> Christus [i.e. Jesus Christ], suffered the extreme penalty during the reign of Tiberius at the hands of one of our procurators, Pontius Pilatus, [in] Judea.[3]

It is likely that Tacitus does not mention the exact form of death penalty (crucifixion) because it was considered to be so gross and base that it was unmentionable in civilized society.

The crunch question is whether or not Jesus came back to life.

Once more the evidence that we have is not restricted to the gospels. Josephus describes how after the crucifixion

> those who had in the first place come to love him did not give up
> their affection for him. On the third day he appeared to them
> restored to life, for the prophets of God had prophesied these and
> countless other marvellous things about him. And the tribe of
> Christians, so called after him, has still to this day not disappeared.[4]

Although this passage is slightly disputed by ancient historians, it is clear that at the least, Josephus knew that Christians claimed that Jesus had come back to life three days after he died.

The crunch question is whether or not Jesus came back to life.

Tacitus also implies that the Christian sect (which he vehemently disliked!) had gained a new lease of life sometime after 'Christus' had been executed. 'The deadly superstition, thus checked for the moment, broke out afresh in Judea, the first source of the evil . . . '[5] He goes on to relate how the movement had spread to Rome, much to his disgust.

These two non-Christian sources (along with others[6]) provide broad support for the claims that are made in the Bible: that Jesus lived, died and rose again. But for more details of the events of that momentous first Easter weekend, we must turn to the records contained in the four biographies of Jesus in the Bible, known as gospels. We must turn back the clock to a Thursday evening.

Evidence from Christian sources[7]
Thursday night: the arrest and trials
On Thursday evening, Jesus shared his last meal with his twelve disciples, in Jerusalem. It was the traditional Jewish Passover meal,

but rather than being the usual celebratory meal remembering God's goodness to Israel, there was a sense of foreboding in the air. Jesus talked of his impending death, and predicted that one of those sharing the meal with him would betray him. After the meal, they walked out of the city to a nearby garden, just across the valley. Jesus prayed in great distress while his disciples fell asleep, exhausted. Late at night, tipped off as to Jesus' whereabouts by Judas (one of Jesus' disciples), some armed servants from the Jewish religious authorities, backed up by a detachment of Roman soldiers, arrested Jesus. After a brief skirmish, Jesus' disciples fled the scene.

The Jewish religious authorities were determined to get rid of Jesus because he was directly challenging their authority, and making illegal blasphemous claims in the process. However, under the occupying Roman forces, they had no power to pass the death penalty, so once they had found Jesus guilty of blasphemy, they then had to persuade the Romans that he was also a political threat to them, and therefore worthy of capital punishment. Thus, after his arrest, Jesus faced several different trials during the night, most of which were probably illegal.

First, he was taken to Annas, the father-in-law of the Jewish high priest, then to Caiaphas, the high priest himself. There was some confusion about the exact charge Jesus was to face, not helped by conflicting witness statements. In the end, the high priest himself asked Jesus, 'Are you the Christ, the Son of the Blessed One?' to which Jesus replied, 'I am.' This claim was clearly blasphemous, and the Sanhedrin (the collective religious leaders who acted as judges) were unanimous in their decision that he was worthy of death.

Friday: the day of execution

The Sanhedrin's middle-of-the-night decisions enabled them to send Jesus to the Roman governor Pontius Pilate, to face charges based around political insurrection – claiming to be 'king of the Jews' could be seen as a political threat to the Romans. However, rather than simply 'rubber-stamping' the Jewish verdict, Pilate procrastinated. He first had Jesus sent to Herod Antipas, the tetrarch of Galilee who happened to be staying nearby, but this trial got them no nearer a decision. Pilate then tried to compromise by offering to flog Jesus before releasing him, but by now the crowds were baying for Jesus' death. Reluctantly, Pilate bowed to their demands, and sentenced Jesus to death.

Before being led to the execution site, Jesus was severely beaten and ridiculed by the soldiers, with a mock crown, made of thorns, jammed on his head. The flogging seems to have weakened Jesus to the point where he was incapable of carrying his own cross on the humiliating parade through Jerusalem to Golgotha, the execution site.

The biblical accounts don't actually describe the process of crucifixion, probably because it was a very common (although extremely brutal) form of the death penalty. The Romans reserved it for the lowest of the low: slaves, violent criminals and those involved in political rebellions. However, the unearthed remains of those executed by crucifixion have revealed that their outstretched arms were nailed to a wooden cross-beam at the wrist, their legs were pushed up to one side and their feet nailed to an upright beam. The resultant effect was that the condemned's arms carried the entire body weight, causing the nails to tear the flesh around the wrist. Eventually, they would die of suffocation, unable to pull themselves up sufficiently to breathe.[8] Despite the extreme pain that Jesus suffered as he was being crucified, he prayed for his executioners, 'Father, forgive them.'

The written charge hung above Jesus' head proclaimed with triumphant disdain, 'This is the king of the Jews.' As Jesus hung on the cross, naked and helpless, the crowds, religious leaders, soldiers and even fellow victims taunted him: 'He saved others, but he can't save himself! Let this Christ, this King of Israel, come down now from the cross, that we may see and believe.'

After about six hours, Jesus died. As if to confirm his death, a soldier pierced Jesus' side with a spear, probably penetrating to the heart.

Normally, the body of the executed person was thrown into a common grave, but a wealthy follower of Jesus, Joseph of Arimathea, asked permission to place his body in a newly-cut, unused tomb, a kind of small cave carved out of rock. The mourners did not have time before nightfall to wash and anoint Jesus' corpse for proper burial according to Jewish custom, so as a temporary measure, the body was wrapped in linen, and packed with a large amount of dry spices. A heavy stone was placed over the tomb's entrance.

Saturday: the day of rest
As the rest of the city continued to celebrate the great national festival of Passover together, Jesus' friends and family were in shock as they tried to come to terms with the events of the previous twenty-four hours, which had unravelled at such great speed. After sundown on the Saturday (the official end of the Jewish Sabbath, with its travel and shopping restrictions), some of the women went to buy spices ready for the Sunday morning, when they planned to wash and anoint Jesus' body properly.

Meanwhile, the religious leaders plotted still further. They had Jesus' words echoing in the minds: 'After three days, I will rise again', and wanted to guard the tomb from attack by his devoted, but distraught, followers. Jesus' former popularity also meant that it was likely that his tomb would become a place for crowds to gather and mourn. Therefore, they went to Pilate and persuaded him that it would be expedient to station a guard at the tomb. The guard would probably have involved between four and sixteen men.

Sunday: the day of surprises[9]

As early as they could, the anointing parties set off for the tomb, to finish preparing Jesus' body for its final rest, wondering how they were going to move the massive stone from the tomb's entrance. They need not have worried. It seems that as they came near, an earthquake occurred which dislodged the stone. The women who entered the tomb saw an angel who announced to them, 'Jesus, who was crucified . . . is not here; he has risen, just as he said.' The angel then told the women to 'see the place [within the tomb] where he lay', after which the women ran away. Soon afterwards, Peter and John also verified that the corpse was gone, leaving the linen burial cloths behind.

John's biography of Jesus records that Mary Magdalene was the first to meet the risen Jesus, although in her grief, she mistook him at first for the gardener before recognizing him. Shortly afterwards, the group of women who had seen the angel at the empty tomb met Jesus. On both occasions, Jesus told the women to tell the other disciples the good news.

Peter and John verified that the corpse was gone.

Peter seems to have been next to meet the risen Jesus, although the location is not recorded. On the Sunday afternoon, Jesus joined two dejected disciples on the road out of Jerusalem to a nearby village, although they too did not recognize him at first. When they did, Jesus disappeared from their sight, and they ran back to

Jerusalem to announce their news to the larger group. As they were reporting their encounter, Jesus appeared in the room, and showed the gathered disciples the scars in his hands and his side. They still could not quite believe that it was not a ghost they were seeing, so Jesus invited them to touch him, and he ate some food with them.

The next forty days: further appearances
No more appearances by the risen Jesus are recorded until the following Sunday when he appeared again to the gathered disciples, this time with Thomas in attendance. Thomas had been absent from the appearances the previous Sunday, and was highly sceptical of the other disciples' excited stories, saying, 'Unless I see the nail marks in his hands and put my finger where the nails were, and put my hand into his side, I will not believe it.' When Jesus appeared, he invited Thomas to do exactly that, and Thomas believed.

Other accounts of Jesus' appearances after his death and resurrection include to seven of the disciples who were fishing on a lake, where he again ate with them; to over five hundred of his followers at the same time in an unspecified location; to the eleven disciples on a hillside; to James (Jesus' brother) by himself; and to all the disciples together again as he was taken back up into heaven. In total, twelve separate appearances of the risen Jesus are recorded in the Bible.

It is important to note that no records state that Jesus died a second time. The disciples firmly believed that Jesus' resurrection body was a transformed one, which was both different and similar to his pre-crucifixion body. For example, he was sometimes difficult to recognize at first, yet clearly still bore scars from the crucifixion. Similarly, he apparently appeared and disappeared at will, yet he could still be touched and perform normal actions like eating. The main difference was that Jesus' body was no longer susceptible to death. These differences mark out Jesus' resurrection from the accounts of those whom Jesus resuscitated from death,[10] for there is no mention of those individuals' bodies being in any way different from their original bodies, and they died a second time. The disciples clearly believed that Jesus was still alive as he ascended into heaven, forty days after the Easter weekend. Thus, Jesus was also able to make a unique appearance to Saul of Tarsus a year or two later.[11]

This chapter has recounted the bare bones of the Christian claim: that Jesus died and rose again. But should these records be classified as fact or fiction? And what of Jesus' bones: is he dead or alive?

7. Is the evidence reliable?

The previous chapter presented a summary of the Bible's account of Jesus' death and subsequent appearances alive again. These are the eyewitness reports from which we must try to work out whether or not Jesus really did rise from the dead. Before we do that, it is right to ask whether the records that we have are *reliable* records. In a court of law, the judge and jury will assess the reliability of a witness's testimony before letting it influence their overall verdict. If the Bible's accounts are not reliable, there is little point carrying on with our enquiry.

Let me give some brief answers to the most common questions people ask about the gospels.

Weren't the four gospels written many years after the events?
Scholars debate exactly when the four gospels were finished, but it is most likely that they were written between thirty and sixty years after Jesus' death and resurrection.[1] That sort of timescale is a relatively safe one for general historical reliability. For example, at the turn of the twenty-first century, there have been one or two

historians who have tried to deny many of the details of the Second World War holocaust of the early 1940s. But it has been a simple matter for the remaining survivors of those horrendous atrocities to put the records straight and discredit the revisionist historians.

Similarly, if the gospel accounts (published within sixty years of the events described) were inaccurate, the documents would have been hotly disputed both by Christians and those who opposed the new movement. When Paul wrote that more than five hundred people saw Jesus alive again after his crucifixion, he implicitly challenged his readers to authenticate his claim with those witnesses – most of whom were still alive.[2]

The material in the finished gospels was not 'new'.

Furthermore, although the gospels may not have been finished until up to sixty years after the events they describe, the individual stories and sayings in the gospels were widely known long before they were written down.

- To begin with, the stories would have been passed on accurately by word of mouth. (Many of the first Christian leaders were Jews who were well practised at accurately memorizing large portions of religious material, unlike most modern Westerners.)[3]
- Next, scholars are virtually unanimous that the stories would have been collated and written down in short collections, which would have circulated widely.[4]
- Only after that would the gospels themselves have been written as well-crafted, finished products.

Thus, the material in the finished gospels was not 'new'; the writers merely collected, refined and carefully structured the already well-known stories for a wider audience. The fact that their gospels were published between thirty and sixty years after the events they described does not automatically make them unreliable; their accuracy should be judged on the quality of their research and the reliability of their sources. Let's look briefly at the individual gospels.

Mark's Gospel

It seems likely that Mark's Gospel was the first to be finished, and that he had Peter (a close friend of Jesus and eyewitness of many of the events) as his main source. So although Mark wasn't a witness himself of most of the events, his main source certainly was. Mark was not relying on hearsay, but a direct eyewitness.

Matthew's Gospel

Matthew's Gospel was probably written by one of Jesus' twelve disciples, so is largely an eyewitness account. Matthew supplemented his own evidence with other written sources (probably including Mark's Gospel), and tailored his material to suit a Jewish audience, but that does not make it less reliable: every biographer has a particular 'target audience' in mind.

John's Gospel

John's Gospel was also probably written by one of Jesus' closest friends, providing further eyewitness details. It may well have been the last gospel to be written, and is notably different in style to the other three gospels. He includes far fewer stories, preferring to add more detail to particular encounters Jesus had with individuals and concentrating on particular teachings Jesus gave. A moderate amount of his content isn't found in the other gospels, but again that doesn't necessarily mean it's fabricated; far more likely is that John had seen the other gospels and knew he didn't need to repeat what they'd already recorded. It would be like trying to publish a new biography of Sir Winston Churchill today, when so many already exist: to be widely distributed, it would need to include what the marketing department might label as 'exclusive new material'.

Luke's Gospel

The introduction to Luke's Gospel spells out his research method. He makes it clear that he did not see the events himself, but that he 'carefully investigated everything from the beginning' and that he aimed to write 'an orderly account', so that his readers 'may know the certainty' of what they had previously heard. His accounts are based on recollections that 'were handed down to us by those who from the first were eye-witnesses.'[5] Luke sounds like a model historian, and as we read on, we see that he is.

Uniquely for a New Testament writer, Luke is at pains to set his material in the context of Roman imperial history, naming different emperors, political events, leading members of the Jewish priestly caste and a host of Roman governors and members of royal families. Professor F.F. Bruce, in his classic work on the reliability of the New Testament documents, pointed out that: 'A writer who thus relates his story to the wider context of world history is courting trouble if he is not careful; he affords his critical readers so many opportunities for testing his accuracy. Luke takes this risk, and stands the test admirably.'[6] Bruce then details the manifold ways in which Luke satisfies the closet historical scrutiny, concluding:

> A man whose accuracy can be demonstrated in matters where we are able to test it is likely to be accurate even where the means for testing him are not available. Accuracy is a habit of mind, and we know from happy (or unhappy) experience that some people are habitually accurate just as others can be depended upon to be inaccurate. Luke's record entitles him to be regarded as a writer of habitual accuracy.[7]

Another professor of classics has concluded that 'Luke is a consummate historian, to be ranked in his own right with the great writers of the Greeks.'[8]

Is there any other evidence to support the gospel materials?

In the previous chapter, I described how the non-Christian ancient writers Tacitus and Josephus both directly mention Jesus' life and death and at least imply the Christian claim of his resurrection. But how have the more specific details found in the gospels been authenticated?

Several other ancient writers refer to Christians and their practices, but Josephus' *Antiquities of the Jews* is the best source for external verification of the New Testament. He mentions many significant characters from the New Testament including detail about John the Baptist's work and death at the hands of Herod.[9] He also mentions Annas and Caiaphas, the high priests who were involved in Jesus' trial, and Felix and Festus, two Roman leaders who legally tried Paul a few decades later, details of which are found in the sequel to Luke's biography of Jesus, a history of the early church known as 'Acts'.[10] Similarly, Tacitus mentions Pontius Pilate, the Governor of Judea who authorized Jesus' execution.[11] These writings confirm that many of the descriptions given to the key religious and political leaders mentioned in the New Testament are accurate.

> Sources outside the gospels have
> helped to verify the detail found
> within the gospels.

Archaeological research has also supported many of the geographical details mentioned in the New Testament, which were previously questioned. For example, in the 1960s, an archaeological dig confirmed that there was indeed a settlement in Nazareth (where the gospels record that Jesus grew up) in the first century – previously, it was thought there hadn't been one. Another modern discovery has been the Pool of Bethesda near the Sheep Gate in the

Old Wall of Jerusalem, which John's Gospel specifies as having five sides.[12] Excavations have confirmed this rare structure.

These brief examples, taken from among many possible examples,[13] show that sources outside the gospels have largely helped to verify the detail found within the gospels. Many other details in the gospels have received external confirmation, indicating that they are reliable accounts.

How reliable are the copies of the gospels we have today?

Even if the *original* gospels were accurate portrayals of the events of Jesus' life, many people wonder whether the *copies* we have today are at all similar to the original versions, or whether they have been mis-copied through the centuries. After all, it's not as if thousands of copies were printed simultaneously; all manuscripts had to be painstakingly copied by hand, allowing plenty of room for human error.

The two main criteria by which scholars judge the reliability of surviving ancient manuscripts are:

1. How many ancient copies of the document do we have?
2. What is the time-span between the original document and the earliest surviving copy?

Under these criteria, it is instructive to compare the four biblical biographies of Jesus with other ancient historical works. Tacitus' *Histories* (written a few decades later than most of the New Testament) has two ancient copies in existence, which were made about seven hundred years after the original. Caesar's *Gallic War* (written one hundred years or so before the New Testament) has ten ancient copies in existence, the earliest of which was made about nine hundred years after the original. Both of these books are accepted by ancient historians as broadly accurate.

By way of contrast, there are 5,000 ancient portions of the New Testament in the original Greek language, and up to 20,000 portions in Latin and other languages. The earliest fragment of

John's Gospel is dated AD 130; and copies of the entire New Testament are dated to about AD 350, a mere three hundred years after the originals were written.

Reviewing these figures, if the surviving copies of Tacitus' *Histories* and Caesar's *Gallic War* are accepted as broadly reliable (on the two criteria mentioned above), then the surviving copies of the New Testament must be accepted as incredibly reliable. Importantly, all the various ancient copies of the gospels in existence have substantial agreement between them, indicating that they are extremely reliable copies of the original version of the gospels.

Why are there apparent discrepancies between the Easter weekend accounts in the different gospels?

A careful reading of the four gospel accounts side by side will reveal some differences. For example:

- not all of the gospels record all the different trials that Jesus faced;
- only Matthew records the earthquake on the Sunday morning;
- the gospels disagree over details such as the number of angels present at the tomb;
- none of the gospels record all of the resurrection appearances.

Many people suppose that this means the gospel records are unreliable.

The police would distrust two witnesses who gave absolutely identical stories about a suspicious event.

In fact, quite the opposite is the case. Today, the police would distrust two witnesses who gave absolutely identical stories about a suspicious event. Similarly, if all of the gospels were identical in what they reported, with no discrepancies, we would surmise that they had deliberately corroborated their stories. Witnesses to any unusual event will have minor differences in what they report, because they will have seen things from different angles, and conferred with different people. One judge puts it this way:

> Courts expect that evidence given by honest and reliable witnesses
> will agree in substance but differ in detail, and they view with
> suspicion witnesses who give the same evidence word for word.
> This always suggests that they have put their heads together to
> make up the story.[14]

Such differences in detail but agreements in substance can be seen elsewhere in ancient history. For example, three ancient historians who wrote about the Great Fire of Rome in AD 64 disagree about where Nero was during the fire, and what he was doing (either singing or playing an instrument). Yet today, no-one questions that there was a fire, and all agree that Nero shirked his responsibilities by making music while the fire raged.

When we look at the four different gospel accounts, we discover a high level of agreement on the substance of the events, with only relatively minor discrepancies over detail. Rather than deliberately corroborating their accounts, each gospel writer has drawn on different eyewitness sources, and together they substantiate what each other says. Sir Edward Clarke, a former High Court judge, described how 'a truthful witness is always artless and disdains effect'. He continued:

> The Gospel evidence for the resurrection is of this class, and as a lawyer I accept it unreservedly as the testimony of truthful men to facts they were able to substantiate.[15]

Another verdict is given by Professor Simon Greenleaf, one of the most influential American legal minds, who played a major part in the development of Harvard Law School's coveted reputation. His series *A Treatise on the Law of Evidence* was a standard text for many years, and put him in good stead to evaluate the varying testimonies concerning Jesus' death and resurrection. His conclusion was that

> There is enough of a discrepancy to show that there could have been no previous concert among them; and at the same time such substantial agreement as to show that they all were independent narrators of the same great transaction.[16]

Other factors in the gospel accounts also point to their authenticity. For example, several events are recorded that would have appeared to the original audience to be detrimental to their overall credibility, such as when one of Jesus' closest friends, Peter (who later became one of the top leaders in the early Church), is reported as having denied knowing Jesus three times.[17] As the gospels were circulated among the first Christians, this story could either have been deliberate and unfounded slander, or an embarrassingly true account.

To include stories about women was to seriously damage the acceptability of the stories.

Perhaps most significantly, the four gospels are unanimous in their record that it was women who discovered the empty tomb, and who first saw the risen Jesus.[18] Unfortunately, in first-century Jewish society, a woman's testimony was worse than useless, and inadmissible in a court of law. Thus, to include stories about women playing such a prominent role on Easter Sunday was to seriously damage the acceptability of the stories.

The point of these examples is that the writers would never have *invented* aspects to the story that would have *undermined* their claims – leading us to conclude that those aspects of the story are true. These seemingly incidental factors in the gospel accounts all help to verify their overall accuracy.

What about the other gospels and the Dead Sea Scrolls etc.?
The blockbuster novel and film *The Da Vinci Code* have alerted many people to the existence of other gospels about Jesus besides the four that are included in the Bible. One of the novel's 'experts', Sir Leigh Teabing, claims that the Roman Emperor Constantine (c. AD 274–337) 'commissioned and financed a new Bible, which omitted those gospels that spoke of Christ's human traits and embellished those gospels that made him godlike. The earlier gospels were outlawed, gathered up and burned.' Quoting from the (recently rediscovered) *Gospel of Philip*, Teabing says that Jesus married Mary Magdalene, and then quoting from the *Gospel of Mary*, concludes that she was the foremost apostle. Teabing further claims that the happy couple had a child and their dynasty survives even today in France.[19] What are we to make of such claims?

Teabing is right to say that ancient documents were found in 1945 in Egypt at Nag Hammadi, and that further scrolls were found in the years following, now known as the 'Dead Sea Scrolls'. However, real-life scholars tend to agree that the Dead Sea Scrolls were written well *before* Jesus' birth, so although they give us much background information on the religious world into which Jesus came, they can tell us nothing about his life or the history of the Jesus movement. The Nag Hammadi scrolls show us five of the 'Gnostic gospels' (including the *Gospel of Thomas*) that Teabing mentions.

The crucial question is whether the biblical gospels or these Gnostic gospels are more historically accurate in their description of Jesus' life. As we've already seen, a key test of reliability is how soon they were written after the events described.

- The *Gospel of Thomas* (which as with all these Gnostic gospels wasn't actually written by the disciple Thomas, but was falsely claimed to be by him to make it sound authentic) was written around AD 150, and is not a 'gospel' as such, merely a collection of sayings attributed to Jesus. Some of it ties in well with the biblical gospels; some of it is very different.
- The *Gospel of Philip* was written in the early part of the third century AD, and quotes from the New Testament we have today. The passage that is quoted in *The Da Vinci Code* is actually written in Coptic (not Aramaic, as Teabing says), and has lots of gaps in it, meaning that Teabing's quote includes a certain amount of guesswork.
- The *Gospel of Mary* was probably written in the late part of the second century AD, but the copy found at Nag Hammadi is much later, and contradicts another earlier version.

The passage that is quoted in 'The Da Vinci Code' has lots of gaps.

Significantly, all of these 'gospels' were written at least several generations after the four biblical gospels, and this goes a long way to explaining why the Gospels of Matthew, Mark, Luke and John were included in the New Testament, but the Gnostic gospels attributed to Thomas, Philip and others were not. Quite simply, they were written far too late to be eyewitness documents. In addition, while the four biblical gospels have differences, they are clearly four portraits of the same person: Jesus of Nazareth. By contrast, the portraits presented in the Gnostic gospels rarely correspond with each other or with the biblical gospels. Factors like these enabled Christians in the generations after Jesus to distinguish easily between authentic, reliable records (which were then widely circulated and included in the New Testament) and made-up, unreliable records (which were openly suppressed).

Teabing also says that 'the Bible, as we know it today, was collated by Constantine.' In fact, there was widespread agreement on the core books that were to be treated as Scripture by around AD 130, and one ancient parchment reveals that sixty-one out of the sixty-six books in the Bible were already viewed as sacred one hundred years before Constantine was born!

It should be obvious that Teabing isn't the expert that *The Da Vinci Code* makes him out to be. Historically speaking, the biblical gospels are far more reliable.

Verdict: is the evidence reliable?

I've given relatively brief answers to the most common questions about the reliability of the gospel records, but I hope this is enough to help you draw your conclusions.[20] Professional archaeologists, historians and linguists have pored over the evidence in the gospels for years, trying to establish their essential reliability or otherwise. Here are the verdicts of two of those scholars:

> The wealth of [New Testament] manuscripts, and above all the narrow interval of time between the writing and the earliest extant copies, make it by far the best-attested text of any ancient writing in the world.[21]

> The evidence for our New Testament writings is ever so much greater than the evidence for many writings of classical authors, the authenticity of which no one dreams of questioning ... If the New Testament were a collection of secular writings, their authenticity would generally be regarded as beyond all doubt.[22]

It should be clear by now that as we read the pages of Matthew, Mark, Luke and John, we are reading very accurate and reliable accounts of the extraordinary events of the weekend in question. How then do we explain Jesus' empty tomb and resurrection appearances?

8. Dead ... ?

In *The Tomb of God*,[1] Paul Schellenberger and Richard Andrews proposed a conspiracy theory to beat them all. They suggested that Jesus' bones were removed in the twelfth century and now lie buried in south-western France, under tons of rock. It was a best-seller, but that is no guide to its truthfulness. Full of inaccuracies and misinformation, it heaps speculation upon speculation to the point where serious scholars have dismissed it out of hand.

Dan Brown's *The Da Vinci Code*[2] has proven to be even more popular. Translated into dozens of languages and made into a film, it is one of the biggest selling novels ever. Its central thesis – that the church has covered up Jesus' marriage to Mary Magdalene, and that their descendants survive to this day – would indeed be the biggest cover-up of all time. But as we saw in the previous chapter, despite claiming to be accurate in all its descriptions, the book actually includes many historical mistakes, and the theories it proposes (while being very entertaining, and grabbing many headlines) have been quashed by academics. It remains in the fiction section of the library.

If a court of law were investigating what happened to Jesus' body, the jury would have to test the competing explanations against the evidence. That evidence was presented in chapter 6 and we saw that the legal experts pronounced it to be reliable in chapter 7, so we are now in a position to weigh the various theories, and decide which is the most plausible. I'd invite you to take your seat on the jury as the cross-examination begins.

Did Jesus die? Was Jesus' tomb empty? Was Jesus' body removed?

There are three crucial questions that must be asked in turn: Did Jesus die? Was Jesus' tomb empty? Was Jesus' body removed? In this chapter, I will show how the answers to those questions spawn the various theories about what really happened to Jesus. Members of the jury may deliberate for as long as they need, but finally must give an answer to each question.

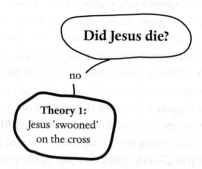

Did Jesus die?

no

Theory 1: Jesus 'swooned' on the cross

Theory 1: Jesus didn't die, but 'swooned' on the cross and later revived
Barbara Thiering suggests in *Jesus the Man*[3] that Jesus didn't die. Rather, he was drugged on the cross to make it *look* as though he

had died, when in fact he had survived. Indeed, she says, so had the two people crucified alongside him (whom she identifies as Judas Iscariot and Simon Magus), even though the gospels tell us that they had had their legs broken, which would have ensured a swift end to their agony. She speculates that all three of them were put in a cave, where Simon Magus was able to give Jesus a cure for the poison he had taken on the cross – conveniently found in the spices which the women had placed in the tomb. Thus, Jesus was able to emerge from the tomb, having apparently died.

While the variations of this theory are new, the gist of it has been around for at least two hundred years. Sometimes it is called the 'swoon theory', as it suggests that Jesus did not really die on the cross, but merely fainted as the intense daytime heat soaked up what stamina remained after his cruel flogging. According to this general theory, the cool of the tomb helped to revive him, so that his appearances three days later were not the appearances of a resurrected man, but merely of a man who came perilously close to death but fortunately survived.

What happened next is anybody's guess. Thiering's book (in true headline-grabbing style) suggests that Jesus was married to Mary Magdalene, had three children, divorced her, then married again, eventually dying some time in his sixties. More reverently, the Ahmadiyya Muslim sect, who also believe that Jesus escaped from the tomb alive, suggest that Jesus died at the age of 120 in North India, being buried in Kashmir in the tomb of an unknown sheikh.

The main problem with such swoon theories it that they have to pick and choose which parts of the earliest historical records to accept, and which to ignore. Consequently, no serious academics accept these theories. One leading scholar concluded that 'believing the accounts in the gospels is child's play compared with believing Thiering's reconstruction.'[4]

It is also very hard to accept that Jesus did not die on the cross. His Roman executioners were battle-hardened soldiers who were familiar with death, and experts in inflicting the death penalty.

Inflicting pain was their speciality, and crucifixion was a routine part of their job. Even before Jesus was taken to the execution site, he had been severely flogged. If you have seen Mel Gibson's film *The Passion of the Christ*, you may remember how severe this beating was. It was almost certainly harsh enough to leave Jesus unable to carry his own cross through Jerusalem.[5]

Evidence that supports the assertion that Jesus died includes:

- As the Jewish authorities wanted the victims dead and buried before the Sabbath started, the executioners broke the victims' legs, leaving them unable to push themselves up to breathe. Death by suffocation would have followed quickly. However, when they came to break Jesus' legs, they saw that he was already dead.[6]

- To confirm and guarantee this, one of the soldiers pierced Jesus' side with a spear, drawing blood and water.[7] This wound would have been enough in itself to kill Jesus in his weakened state, but the flow of blood and water is medical evidence that he had already died.[8]

- Jesus' death was unusually quick, causing Pilate to double-check with the centurion that Jesus had already died. The duty centurion confirmed Jesus' death.[9]
- The execution squad had a vested interest in ensuring that Jesus was dead: it is likely that they would have suffered the death penalty themselves had they let one of their victims escape with their life.

When these factors are weighed together, by far the most logical conclusion is that Jesus died. However, if by some miracle Jesus had survived the crucifixion, the 'swoon' theory has further difficulties. For example:

- Jesus clearly would have needed expert medical help, yet none could have come from outside the tomb because of the sealed entrance and Roman guards. There would not even have been any food or water inside the tomb. The eyewitness evidence tells us that Jesus was buried alone in a fresh tomb[10] – not with other people who could have helped him revive!
- Jesus would need to have escaped from his grave clothes. This would have been very difficult as they probably would have hardened around him into a mummy-like effect.
- Jesus would need to have escaped from the tomb – somehow moving the boulder from the entrance. The boulder was far too heavy for one fit man to move, let alone a man weakened by severe flogging and failed crucifixion.
- Jesus would need to have crept past the Roman soldiers who were guarding the tomb, without being noticed.
- Having *escaped* death by the narrowest of margins, Jesus would need to have convinced his followers that he had *triumphed* over death, showing no ill effects. One ardent sceptic admitted that this was 'impossible', saying, 'Such a

resuscitation could by no possibility have changed the [disciples'] sorrow into enthusiasm, and elevated their reverence into worship.'[11]

These improbabilities further support the conclusion that the 'swoon theory' is implausible. Jesus could not have survived the best attentions of his executioners; he really did die on the cross. This brings us to our second key question: was Jesus' tomb empty on the Sunday morning?

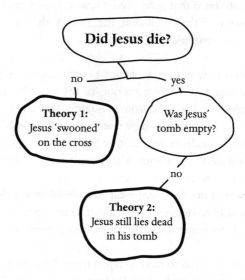

Theory 2: Jesus still lies dead in his tomb

Given that Jesus died, it is not unnatural to assume that his corpse remained, and still remains, in his tomb. Indeed, a BBC programme in the mid-1990s highlighted the discovery in Jerusalem of a first-century ossuary (a casket for bones) with the engraving 'Jesus son of Joseph' on it. Also in the same tomb were ossuaries of people named Joseph, Mary, and Judah, a 'son of Jesus'. However, these names were all very common in first-century Israel, and although the media made a big fuss about the discovery, the professional archaeologists knew that it was a bit like finding an entry for John and Jane Smith in a telephone directory. It no more proved that Jesus' body remained in his tomb than did the Turin Shroud.

The disciples accidentally looked in the wrong tomb

Some people suggest that Jesus' followers were mistaken in thinking that Jesus' tomb was empty because they were looking in the wrong tomb. However, looking at the eyewitness evidence reveals that several different groups of people knew where the correct tomb was, and would have been able to identify it.

- Mark's biography states very clearly that Mary Magdalene was there when Jesus' body was laid in the tomb on the Friday evening, and that she was also one of the women who went to the tomb early on the Sunday morning.[12] To claim that her grief made her forget within forty-eight hours where her dear friend was buried is deeply patronizing!
- Joseph of Arimathea is even less likely to have forgotten the tomb in which Jesus was placed, because he owned it.[13]

- The Roman guards who were stationed at the tomb would not have left it once stationed there.[14]

To suppose that the tomb was not actually empty asks us to believe that *all* of these groups of people got the venue wrong, despite their vested interests in getting the right tomb. For example, if Jesus' friends and followers had got the wrong tomb, we can be certain that both the Roman and Jewish authorities would have been delighted to correct their mistake quickly.

Furthermore, if this theory was right, and Jesus was still lying dead and buried elsewhere, we would also have to find adequate explanations for the disciples' strong conviction that they had seen Jesus alive again – which is easier said than done (see Theory 4 below). All in all, it is highly implausible to believe that Jesus' tomb still had his corpse lying in it. A well-respected Jewish scholar reached this conclusion:

> In the end, when every argument has been considered and weighed, the only conclusion acceptable to the historian must be ... that the women who set out to pay their last respects to Jesus found to their consternation, not a body, but an empty tomb.[15]

The disciples deliberately made up the story about Jesus' tomb being empty

Some people suggest that the disciples knew full well that Jesus' body was still in the tomb and made up the story about it being empty. This questions the reliability of the gospels' records, which contradicts the conclusions of the previous chapter. But there are other problems with this view as well, most of which will be expanded on later in this chapter.

- Advocates of this theory would still need to find convincing explanations for over five hundred people seeing Jesus alive after his death.

- The authorities would have gladly silenced the new movement by exhuming the body. That they did not is strong evidence that they could not.
- It is hard to imagine that the disciples could possibly have convinced people that Jesus was alive again if they knew that he was still dead – yet they convinced thousands.
- It is even harder to imagine that the disciples would have been willing to die a martyr's death for a cause they knew to be false – yet many of them did die for their convictions. Today, suicide bombers are prepared to die for what they *believe* to be *true* (whether or not it actually *is* true). But no one is stubborn enough to die for what they *know* to be *false*. In any case, such a huge cover-up would have been impossible to maintain, as Charles Colson, lawyer and special counsel to President Richard Nixon knows only too well, having been imprisoned for his part in the Watergate scandal:

> Take it from one who was inside the Watergate web looking out, who saw firsthand how vulnerable a cover-up is: Nothing less than a witness as awesome as the resurrected Christ could have caused those men to maintain to their dying whispers that Jesus is alive and Lord.[16]

No-one is stubborn enough to die for what they know to be false.

The thousands of people who converted to Christianity after the disciples started preaching about the resurrection were all Jews who either lived locally, or were visiting. One scholar comments that these people

> were accepting a revolutionary teaching which could have been discredited by taking a few minutes' walk to a garden just

outside the city walls. Far from discrediting it, they one and all enthusiastically spread it far and wide. Every one of those first converts was a proof of the empty tomb, for the simple reason that they could never have become disciples if that tomb had still contained the body of Jesus.[17]

For all these reasons, it is most improbable that the disciples could have invented the story of the tomb being empty: it is again best to conclude that Jesus' tomb was indeed empty by the Sunday morning. But how did it come to be empty? Our final key question is this: was Jesus' body removed?

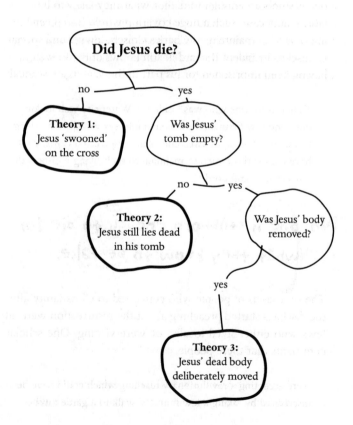

Did Jesus die?

no — yes

Theory 1: Jesus 'swooned' on the cross

Was Jesus' tomb empty?

no — yes

Theory 2: Jesus still lies dead in his tomb

Was Jesus' body removed?

yes

Theory 3: Jesus' dead body deliberately moved

Theory 3: The tomb was empty because someone moved Jesus' body

Given that Jesus was really dead when he was placed in the tomb and that all the evidence points to his tomb being empty on the Sunday morning, many suggest that Jesus did not rise to life again, but that his corpse was removed.

A variety of different groups of people, each with their own motives, have been suggested as the possible culprits.

Grave-robbers stole the body

Grave-robbing was not unknown in ancient times, and with thousands of visitors to Jerusalem for the Passover, there were bound to be more undesirables than usual. With Pilate having posted the sign 'King of the Jews' over Jesus' head as he died, some might have been enticed by the (incorrect!) thought that the king's grave would have contained riches.

There are several improbabilities with this theory:

- It is unlikely that robbers would have managed to pass the professional Roman guards on duty at the tomb who would have faced severe punishment for allowing the robbers in.

- Why would the robbers have stolen a worthless corpse from the tomb, and left the valuable burial cloths behind?[18] They would have been fairly incompetent thieves!
- Again, an explanation would still be needed for the disciples' meetings with Jesus after his death, and the subsequent changes in their lives.

This theory has no evidence to support it, and plenty weighing against it.

The disciples removed the body

Some people suppose that the disciples were expecting Jesus to rise again, and so suggest that the disciples removed the body to try to 'engineer' Jesus' resurrection for him.

In 1992, the well-known biographer A.N. Wilson turned his attention to Jesus,[19] and proposed a variation to this theory. Having dealt with Jesus' life and death, Wilson suggests that he remained dead, and his disciples took his body back to Galilee for burial there. Wilson goes on to attempt to explain the rise of the Christian movement by suggesting that Jesus' brother James reassured Jesus' followers that it had all happened 'according to the Scriptures', and was in the process mistaken for Jesus himself – as his brother, there could have been a strong family resemblance. It was after this case of mistaken identity that the story spread that Jesus had risen from the dead.

As we will see in a moment, there are huge obstacles to believing that the disciples could have taken Jesus' body, but in response to Wilson's particular theory, there are also massive historical barriers to believing that James could have been mistaken for Jesus. According to the first historians of the church, James himself was a key player in the early years,[20] and it is inconceivable that he would have let such a crucial misunderstanding linger. In any case, James is listed as one of the people to whom Jesus appeared,[21] so Wilson has to conveniently ignore that piece of historical data as well.

There are huge obstacles to believing that the disciples could have taken Jesus' body.

Wilson's is an imaginative idea, but does not stand up to historical investigation. One scholar begins his critique of Wilson's portrait of Jesus by saying, 'This is, frankly, such a tissue of nonsense that it is hard to know where to begin to answer it.'[22]

So what are the other problems with the notion that the disciples moved Jesus' body from its tomb? For starters, it is clear from the subsequent reactions of the disciples that they were *not* expecting Jesus to come back to life, so 'engineering' his resurrection would have been the last thing to enter his followers' distraught minds.

Nevertheless, that the disciples stole the body was the 'official' explanation that was given by the Temple authorities. Matthew's biography of Jesus records that some of the guards from the tomb

> went into the city and reported to the chief priests everything that had happened [i.e. the empty tomb]. When the chief priests had met with the elders and devised a plan, they gave the soldiers a large sum of money, telling them, 'You are to say, "His disciples came during the night and stole him away while we were asleep." If this report gets to the governor, we will satisfy him and keep you out of trouble.' So the soldiers took the money and did as they were instructed. And this story has been widely circulated among the Jews to this very day.[23]

As an explanation, it was pretty poor: the highly disciplined Roman guards faced severe discipline for sleeping on duty, and if they *had* all been asleep, how did they know who had taken the body?! And would they really have slept through several men shifting a massive boulder right next to them? Matthew doesn't even bother to attack this particular explanation because it was so laughable.

But could there be any truth behind the story – could the disciples have removed the body? It is highly unlikely, for a number of reasons:

- The disciples had already shown themselves to be a cowardly lot in the face of soldiers, by running away when Jesus was arrested[24] – indeed, most of them seem to have fled Jerusalem itself. Are we now to suppose that the few dejected men who remained were suddenly courageous enough to take on the professionally trained Roman guards, having watched Jesus' gruesome execution? It is highly improbable that they would have taken on the guard, and inconceivable that they would have got past them.
- If they did get past the guard, why were they never charged with the theft of the corpse, which was state property? Merely to have accused the disciples of such theft would have severely dented their subsequent popularity. That such a charge was never made indicates that there was no evidence of it having happened.
- If the disciples did remove the body, but proceeded to proclaim Jesus as risen, they would have been deliberately deceiving their hearers into believing a lie. We've already seen that this is highly unlikely, and in any case, it does not fit well with the rest of their character. (Tacitus and Pliny, two of the Roman historians mentioned in chapter 6, both highlighted the distinctively upright morality of the early Christians.)
- If a few of Jesus' friends did steal the body, a realistic explanation of the resurrection appearances to all the other people would still need to be found (see Theory 4 below).

Personally, I find this the least persuasive of all the theories that have been produced to explain the empty tomb.

The Jewish authorities removed the body
Another group of people who might have had reason to move the body were the Jewish authorities. Maybe they wanted to move it so that Jesus' tomb couldn't become a shrine for his followers? Or in a kind of double-outwitting manoeuvre, maybe they thought that by moving the body, they could prevent Jesus' disciples moving the body and claiming he was alive? But whatever their motives, is it plausible that they moved the body?

Within weeks of Jesus' death and claimed resurrection, thousands of people were switching from a traditional Jewish belief to a belief in Jesus as the Messiah. The Jewish authorities were powerless to stop the new movement: they put the chief proponents in prison and told them to stop preaching, but when released, they just carried on.[25] Eventually, they had to resort to physical violence to try to quell the movement[26] – although even that did not work. Of all the tactics they could have tried to quash the new movement, the one that would have worked would have been the producing of either Jesus' body or witnesses stating that they had removed and destroyed the body. That they did not do this is ample reason to conclude that the Jewish authorities did not remove the body in the first place.

The Roman authorities removed the body
A final group of people who could conceivably have moved the body were the Roman authorities. To them, the 'Jesus movement' obviously had political overtones, with people claiming that he was King of the Jews. The Roman authorities had as much desire as the Jewish ones to clamp down on the new movement, because they feared it would lead to a popular uprising against their brutal occupation. So maybe they moved the body – again to even safer keeping?

But for much the same reasons as if the Jewish authorities had taken the body, it is also highly unlikely that the Roman ones did. As soon as the new movement began gathering pace (which it did very quickly), they could have produced Jesus' corpse and stopped the movement in its tracks. But they did not because they could not.

So was the body moved?
Of all the possible culprits that have been suggested for the removal of Jesus' body, none are convincing. Admittedly, it doesn't seem to make much sense to say that Jesus' tomb was empty but that his body hadn't been removed – we'll come back to that problem at the beginning of the next chapter.

> **Of all the possible culprits that have been suggested for the removal of Jesus' body, none are convincing.**

But quite apart from the weaknesses already exposed in these alternative theories, those who say that Jesus remained dead still have to try to discredit the eyewitness statements of those who claimed to see Jesus alive again. Again, the jury must make up their mind.

Theory 4: The disciples didn't actually see Jesus alive again
Many people have surmised that the disciples did not *actually* see Jesus alive again, they just *thought* they did – in other words, they were hallucinating. After all, it is not uncommon for those who are grieving to think that they have glimpsed or heard their loved one after their death.

But the historical accounts we have of Jesus' appearances do not merely involve people *seeing* him, they also include people *touching* him and *eating* with him.[27] Such physical contact would be

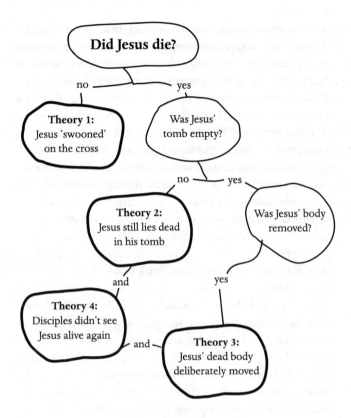

impossible with an hallucination. Further, the appearances do not allow for accepted medical definitions of hallucinations for the following reasons:

- Hallucinations happen to individuals, not groups, yet the gospel records tell us that Jesus tended to appear to groups rather than individuals. For example, he appeared to Cleopas and his companion; to ten of the disciples and then to eleven of them; to a group gathered for breakfast; to five hundred people at once. (The Christian leader Paul who wrote about this latter event did so while most of these witnesses were still alive – so any doubters could have interviewed them all to verify their claims.[28]) If it's highly unlikely that two people would hallucinate the same thing at the same time, it's impossible for five hundred people to hallucinate the same thing at the same time.[29]

○ Hallucinations happen to certain types of individuals. Some people say that Mary Magdalene was sufficiently emotional to hallucinate, and it is true that some people are more susceptible to hallucinations than others. But the resurrection appearances were made to a wide variety of people – men and women; rugged fishermen, wily tax-collectors, seasoned debaters and others. It is too much to suppose that all of these people were vulnerable to hallucinations. Maybe 'Doubting Thomas' was the least likely person to hallucinate, yet even he was very quickly convinced that Jesus had come back to life.[30]

○ Hallucinations happen in certain circumstances. Psychiatrists say that time of day and lighting levels affect the likelihood of hallucinations. Yet Jesus' appearances were very varied in their nature: early morning in a garden; breakfast-time by the sea; in the afternoon in the bright sunlight; in the evening in a crowded room; on top of a mountain during the day. The wide variations in the circumstances make it extremely unlikely that the sightings could all be hallucinations.

○ Hallucinations tend to increase in severity over time, as the condition becomes worse, yet the historical accounts tell us that the sightings of Jesus stopped abruptly after forty days.

No-one expects to see a dead person alive again.

Of course, no-one expects to see a dead person alive again – not even Jesus' friends did. So on one of the first occasions when they saw the resurrected Jesus, it is not surprising that they assumed it was a ghost. But Jesus, knowing their thoughts, said to them, 'Look at my hands and my feet. It is I myself! Touch me and see; a ghost does not have flesh and bones, as you see I have.' Then he showed them his hands and feet, and proceeded to eat some fish with them.[31] Jesus' friends might have thought to themselves that they were hallucinating at first, but because they saw Jesus several times, and because his appearances were so tangible, they soon became convinced that they were not just 'seeing things' – but that Jesus really had come back from the dead.

Together, these factors all point to the conclusion that the appearances to the disciples cannot simply be dismissed as hallucinations.

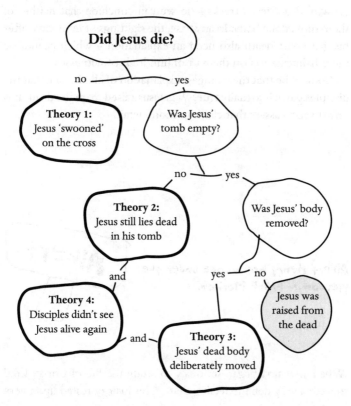

Conclusion

What happened after Jesus was sentenced to death? We've examined the competing theories but all of them have been found wanting. We can be sure that Jesus did die on the cross on the Friday afternoon, yet that by Sunday morning, his tomb was empty. It is extremely unlikely that grave-robbers or the disciples could have taken the body from under the watchful eyes of the Roman guard, and even if they did, it would not explain the radical change in behaviour of the disciples. If either the Roman or Jewish authorities had removed the body, they would quickly have brought forward either witnesses or the corpse itself as sufficient proof to undermine the new movement's claims and stop its growth 'dead' in its tracks – so we can conclude that neither of them moved the body. In any case, the sightings of Jesus alive after his gruesome death also need an explanation – which cannot be mere hallucination on the part of hundreds of witnesses.

Could it be that the strangest explanation of all, the one that the disciples gave, is actually true? Was Jesus raised from the dead? It is now time to assess that claim in more detail.

real lives

Albert Henry Ross wrote under the pseudonym Frank Morison.

'When ... I first began seriously to study the life of Christ, I did so with a very definite feeling that ... his history rested upon very insecure foundations.' Ross was particularly dubious that the miracles really happened. He set out to write a book on the period of time immediately before and after Jesus' death, aiming to 'strip [the story] of its overgrowth of primitive beliefs and dogmatic suppositions'.[32]

However, when he came to investigate the events closely (a task he did so rigorously that many wrongly assumed he was a lawyer), he became convinced that the gospel records were reliable, leading him to the surprising conclusion that 'There certainly is a deep and profoundly historical basis to [the statement] "The third day he rose again from the dead." '[33]

Ross became especially dismissive of the idea that the key witnesses deliberately made the story up. 'No great moral structure like the early church, characterised as it was by lifelong persecution and personal suffering, could have reared its head on a statement every one of the eleven apostles knew to be a lie.'[34]

The book he eventually published became a classic. He tells his story in its Preface:

'This study is . . . the inner story of a man who originally set out to write one kind of book and found himself compelled by the sheer force of circumstances to write quite another.

'It is not that the facts themselves altered, for they are recorded imperishably . . . in the pages of human history. But the interpretation to be put upon the facts underwent a change. Somehow the perspective shifted – not suddenly, as in a flash of insight or inspiration, but slowly, almost imperceptibly, by the very stubbornness of the facts themselves.'[35]

9. or Alive?

Some of the theories that have been put forward to explain away the disciples' claims about the mysterious events of the first Easter were examined in chapter 8. But the more the alternative explanations are tested, the more they seem to confirm the bare facts of the case:

- that Jesus died on the cross on the Friday afternoon;
- that Jesus' corpse was laid in a tomb belonging to Joseph of Arimathea, shortly before sunset on the Friday;
- that Jesus' tomb was empty on the Sunday morning;
- that Jesus' followers and friends believed that they subsequently saw him alive again;
- that Jesus' followers and friends were so convinced by what they had seen that they proceeded to persuade thousands of others that Jesus had risen from the dead; and some of them endured martyrdom rather than denounce their beliefs.

Sherlock Holmes is probably the world's most famous fictional detective. Sir Arthur Conan Doyle, his creator, put these words in his mouth:

> When you have eliminated the impossible, whatever remains, however improbable, must be the truth.[1]

So far, we have eliminated the explanations proposed in the previous chapter. But is the explanation of the disciples – that Jesus bodily rose from the dead – actually possible? This chapter will look at some further objections that are commonly raised against the resurrection, before calling on some 'expert witnesses' for their opinions.

'The resurrection is scientifically impossible'

I was talking with a Chinese friend of mine one day about the resurrection, and he said to me, 'But I just can't believe it – biologically!' Indeed, it does sound incredible – that a person who has been declared dead by his executioners should come back to life. It implies a staggering reversal of the laws of nature, such as never has been seen since. Our experience of this world is that dead men do not rise, so surely it is impossible that Jesus could have risen?

Imagine you are in a science lab in school, doing an experiment. You come to plot a graph as you are writing up, and it turns out your results have a perfect correlation, with just one wild aberration. What do you do: do you discount the aberration, thinking that you probably made a mistake somewhere in your methodology, or that your equipment was faulty, drawing the conclusion that there is a perfect correlation without exception? I dare say many a school pupil has done that! But an experienced scientist would have to conclude that there is not quite a perfect correlation. There is an exception to the rule.

Proper scientific enquiry is based around the testing of an hypothesis by experiment, the results of which are then analysed

before drawing conclusions. If we analyse what happens when people die, there are millions of instances of people staying dead. But there is one wild aberration. There is an exception to the rule.

Thus, it is bad science to say that 'dead men don't rise, therefore Jesus can't have risen', presuming to ignore a certain piece of data because it does not fit in with the conclusion trying to be reached. Indeed, to believe that any miracle *can't* happen is as much an act of faith as to believe that it *can* happen, because it requires an unprovable belief that there are no supernatural forces within the universe.

Jesus' resurrection, by its very nature, claims to be a unique event which cannot be repeated. In this sense, it is like all 'miracles' – scientifically untestable. R.J. Berry, who for twenty-two years was a professor of genetics at University College London, wrote on behalf of fourteen eminent Christian scientists that

> Miracles are unprecedented events. Whatever the current fashions in philosophy or the revelations of opinion polls may suggest, it is important to affirm that science (based as it is upon the observation of precedents) can have nothing to say on the subject. Its 'laws' are only generalisations of our experience.[2]

It must be concluded that while science cannot *prove* Jesus' resurrection, it cannot *dis*prove it either. (Similarly, while some scientists such as Richard Dawkins are adamant that there is no supernatural force in our universe, it is not really within science's remit to pronounce on such matters. As it happens, many scientists do believe in God.[3])

> **While science cannot prove Jesus' resurrection, it cannot disprove it either.**

In fact, if Jesus *did* rise from the dead, it is evidence that he was not merely a normal human being like you or I. Christians claim that Jesus shared God's nature as well as ours, and it is certainly clear from the records that the quality of his life was remarkably different to everyone else's. As one author puts it:

> He lived an unsullied life, one that not even his detractors could credibly slander, one that even his judge could not fault. How can we be certain that a perfect life which had given no foothold to sin might not also master death, which scripture asserts is in some mysterious way connected with sin? We have no other example of the 'sinless' category to compare Jesus with. There are no parallels by which to measure the possibility of his unique rising from death. It ill befits the competent scientist or the open minded enquirer to say 'It could not have happened'.[4]

'But it simply can't be true!'

Many people object to the claim of the resurrection on similar grounds, but from a philosophical point of view, rather than from a scientific one. Any miracle, and certainly an event such as a resurrection, would contravene all laws of physics and nature, which we know from observation to be true. They conclude, therefore, that events which break these laws of nature cannot happen. For them, to believe in such un-provable exceptions to the rules is 'intellectual suicide'.

Sometimes it is suggested that people who lived in Jesus' day were less intellectually advanced than our generation, and therefore more susceptible to believing in miracles. However, that wasn't Paul's experience when preaching to philosophers in Athens. As soon as he mentioned Jesus' resurrection, 'some of them sneered'.[5] Intelligent people ridiculed the idea of a resurrection on first hearing two thousand years ago, just as many do today. Besides, Jesus' followers didn't claim that *lots* of people rose unaided from the dead, they claimed it was *unique* – which is precisely why they made such a noise about Jesus' resurrection.

Just because an event does not *normally* happen does not mean that it could *never* happen. If everything that happens in the world needs a natural explanation, then nothing supernatural can be allowed. Yet there are many people in the world who would testify to having seen events with no natural explanation. And if this universe did come into being by the will of some creative force, rather than by pure chance, it is still possible that the creative force can interject again.

> **Just because an event does not normally happen does not mean that it could never happen.**

This is what Christians claim – that God was intimately involved in the creation of the universe, and is still intimately involved in the continued life of the universe. He has set in place the laws of nature by which we exist, and scientists have analysed how those laws of nature work. But occasionally God chooses to work in ways for which we can find no 'natural' explanation. The gospels record Jesus performing many such miracles – the blind seeing, the deaf hearing, the lame walking, even the dead reviving. Not even his opponents doubted that Jesus performed these miracles or that they were supernatural, and certainly the crowds who followed were attracted to him precisely because of the miracles. Could it not be that if Jesus is God, he could heal people instantly? Could it not be that if Jesus is God, the creator of life, he could give new life? As one of the first Christian leaders, Paul, put it, when on trial before a king, 'Why should any of you consider it incredible that God raises the dead?'[6]

Richard Swinburne, Professor of the Philosophy of the Christian Religion at Oxford University, has written a philosophical defence of the existence of God, and of the resurrection of Jesus of Nazareth. He acknowledges that 'The resurrection of Jesus, if it occurred ... would clearly be a violation of natural laws which only God could bring about.'[7] He also suggests, however, that a resurrection is exactly the sort of 'signature' that God would put on Jesus' life if Jesus were indeed God incarnate. In a very technical appendix, he tries to evaluate the mathematical probability that Jesus' resurrection happened, and arrives at a probability of 0.97, explaining:

> In other words our total evidence ... makes it very probable indeed that God became incarnate in Jesus Christ who rose from the dead.[8]

But while philosophical debate about miracles is important, it must be acknowledged that the realm of philosophy, like the realm of science, cannot give us a definite answer on Jesus' resurrection. As a Professor of Law and Humanities put it:

> The only way we can know whether an event *can* occur is to see whether in fact it *has* occurred. The problem of miracles, then, must be solved in the realm of historical investigation, not in the realm of philosophical speculation.[9]

Christians do not say that belief in the resurrection of Jesus is irrational or illogical. As it has never been repeated, it is not experimentally verifiable by science, and as it breaks the laws of nature, we are right to question its occurrence carefully, but the resurrection is certainly still subject to certain rules of evidence, based on the testing of witnesses. Rather than asking scientists and philosophers whether the resurrection *could* have occurred, we would do better to ask historians and lawyers whether they think the resurrection *did* occur.

> **Rather than asking scientists and philosophers whether the resurrection could have occurred, we would do better to ask historians and lawyers whether they think the resurrection did occur.**

Listening to the experts: historians

Historians are trained and experienced in looking at accounts of past events, and assessing the relative credibility of those accounts. Their role is to dismiss one version of events as highly improbable and state that another account is far more likely to be true.

It is not surprising that many historians have examined the birth and growth of the Christian church, starting with examining the life, death and apparent resurrection of Jesus of Nazareth. I have already said that no serious historian doubts that Jesus existed, or that he was executed. But what do they make of the reports of his resurrection?

Drawing conclusions from eyewitness evidence

Paul Maier was a Professor of Ancient History. Underlining the historical likelihood of the empty tomb, he wrote:

If all the evidence is weighed carefully and fairly, it is indeed justifiable, according to the canons of historical research, to conclude that the tomb in which Jesus was buried was actually empty on the morning of the first Easter. And no shred of evidence has yet been discovered in literary sources, epigraphy or archaeology that would disprove this statement.[10]

Professor Thomas Arnold of Oxford University was an expert in Roman history. He went a stage further, affirming not just the empty tomb, but the resurrected Jesus:

> I have been used for many years to studying the histories of other times, and to examine and weigh the evidence of those who have written about them, and I know of no one fact in the history of mankind which is proved by better and fuller evidence of every sort, to the understanding of a fair inquirer, than the great sign which God hath given us that Christ died and rose again from the dead.[11]

These verdicts help build our confidence in the likelihood of the resurrection having happened. However, historians do more than simply assess the likely authenticity of different versions of individual events. They also analyse the links between events, asking what caused something to happen. For example, school pupils learn that the First World War was sparked by the murder of Archduke Franz Ferdinand, but they also learn of the context of increasing tension between countries in the Triple Alliance and those in the Triple Entente. By itself, the Archduke's murder would not have caused the First World War. But, given the existing international tensions, the assassination was sufficient for the countries to line up in defence and attack, and for invasions to begin. It is likely that if the Archduke had not been murdered, there would have been another 'trigger' event before long that would have brought the nations to war.

Drawing conclusions about the 'trigger' event
When analysing records of the years that followed Jesus' death, historians note two unusual patterns, which require some sort of 'trigger': the phenomenal growth of the Jesus movement, and the radical content of their message.

- Within days of Jesus' death, all signs of grief were erased from the faces of Jesus' followers, and within weeks, this tiny leaderless group had grown to number thousands – and they were voluntarily opposing the authorities, by now fearless of the possible consequences. It wasn't long before Stephen became the first Christian martyr, but far from damping down the spread of the movement, it only served to fan its growth out even further.[12]

- Although Jesus had mentioned that he would die and rise again, and although Jews had believed in the idea of 'resurrection' for centuries, it was not a major emphasis in Jesus' teaching or in the current religious climate. In fact, if people believed anything about the resurrection, it was that everyone would be raised at the end of time, not that one man would rise from the dead in the middle of history. In other words, when the disciples preached that Jesus had risen bodily from the dead, this was a revolutionary teaching.[13]

The historian has to ask, 'What event could have triggered these patterns?'

Some people imagine that Jesus' disciples were so caught up in his teaching and miracles that *any* dramatic event would have sparked them into preaching about Jesus and calling people to follow him. Unconvinced that Jesus rose again, these people suggest that it was Jesus' *death*, not his *resurrection*, which was the event that galvanized his disciples into action. However, historians who look at the subsequent growth and message of the church can dismiss this suggestion on the grounds that Jesus' *death* would not have been a sufficient trigger for the disciples' revolutionary message about his *resurrection*.

To return to the parallel with how historians treat the beginning of the First World War: just as the murder of the Archduke by itself was not sufficient provocation for war, so Jesus' death and his empty tomb by themselves would not have been enough to prompt the new message and rapid growth of the church.

Tom Wright has taught at Oxford and Cambridge universities, and is widely regarded as one of the leading authorities on the New Testament and events of those times. Having written an 800-page examination on the background, events and beliefs in the resurrection of Jesus,[14] few people are more qualified to give a reliable assessment of the competing theories and claims about what happened to Jesus' corpse. Comparing the claims of Jesus' first disciples with the theories and proposals of later centuries that we examined in chapter 8, he says:

As far as I am concerned, the historian may and must say that all the other explanations for why Christianity arose, and why it took the shape it did, are far less convincing *as historical explanations* than the one the early Christians themselves offer: that Jesus really did rise from the dead on Easter morning, leaving an empty tomb behind him.

He goes on:

Of course, there are several reasons why people may not want, and often refuse, to believe this. But the historian must weigh, as well, the alternative accounts they themselves offer. And, to date, none of them have anything like the explanatory power of the simple, but utterly challenging, Christian one. The historian's task is not to force people to believe. It is to make it clear that the sort of reasoning historians characteristically employ – inference to the best explanation, tested rigorously in terms of the explanatory power of the hypothesis thus generated – points strongly *towards* the bodily resurrection of Jesus...[15]

Elsewhere, he is even more forthright in his conclusion:

I have come to the conviction that the rise of the early church in the 40s and 50s is completely inexplicable, historically speaking, unless you have a strongly historical, bodily view of the resurrection of Jesus of Nazareth.[16]

Summary
Professional historians:

- affirm that the tomb was empty;
- state that alternative theories to explain the empty tomb are weak;
- affirm that people actually seeing Jesus alive again after his execution is the best explanation for the church's message and growth;
- conclude that Jesus rose from the dead.

But what of our second group of expert witnesses?

Listening to the experts: lawyers

Every day, thousands of verdicts are reached in courts around the world. The verdicts are reached by judges and juries after the hearing and sifting of relevant evidence. What would these people conclude about the events of the first Easter, trained as they are to discern truth from lies and reliable witnesses from false witnesses?

- Sir Edward Clarke wrote:

  As a lawyer I have made a prolonged study of the evidences for the events of the first Easter Day. To me the evidence is conclusive, and over and over again in the High Court I have secured the verdict on evidence not nearly so compelling.[17]

- A former Lord Chief Justice of England, Lord Darling, wrote that concerning the resurrection,

  we are not merely asked to have faith. In its favour as a living truth there exists such overwhelming evidence, positive and negative, factual and circumstantial, that no intelligent jury in the world could fail to bring in a verdict that the resurrection story is true.[18]

- Val Grieve, a lawyer, said:

  I have carefully examined the evidence for the resurrection, the physical return from the dead of Jesus Christ ... I claim that logic must point in the direction of his resurrection on an actual day and date in our history when, if you had been there, you could have touched the living Jesus and heard him speak.[19]

- In a magnificent understatement, Lord Lyndhurst wrote, 'I know pretty well what evidence is' (he was Solicitor General of the British government, Attorney General of Great Britain and three times High Chancellor of England),

'and I tell you, such evidence as that for the resurrection has never broken down yet.'[20]

Again, these experts help boost our confidence in the likelihood of the resurrection accounts being accurate and true.

However, a full examination of the case in a court of law would draw not only on eyewitnesses, but could also draw on 'circumstantial evidence'. One judge likened circumstantial evidence to a rope composed of several cords, explaining:

> One strand of the cord might be insufficient to sustain the weight, but three stranded together may be of quite sufficient strength. Thus ... there may be a combination of circumstances, no one of which would raise a reasonable conviction, or more than a mere suspicion, but the whole, taken together, may create a strong conclusion ... with as much certainty as human affairs can require.[21]

In the case of Jesus' resurrection, such additional evidence, supporting the strong conclusions already outlined above, could include the following:

1. From Sabbath to Sunday

The Jewish holy day, reserved for worship, is the Sabbath, which runs from dusk on Friday to dusk on Saturday. It has been so for thousands of years. Yet very early on, the Christians, who were

If there had merely been an empty tomb, the tone of Sunday worship would be puzzlement and unanswered questions. As it is, the tone is one of joy — at the fact of Jesus' resurrected life.

mostly from Jewish backgrounds, started holding their main gatherings on a Sunday. Millions of Christians around the world since then have gathered on Sundays to worship. What could have prompted this change from Sabbath to Sunday? There is clearly a link with what happened on Easter Sunday – the discovery of the empty tomb, and the resurrection appearances. If there had merely been an empty tomb, the tone of Sunday worship would be puzzlement and unanswered questions. As it is, the tone is one of joy – at the fact of Jesus' resurrected life.

2. Jesus has remained significant for 2000 years

The ancient world was littered with religious movements and sects, much as today's cities are. In Jesus' time, the Jewish religion had sects known as the Pharisees, the Sadducees and the Essenes. Yet none of these sects remain. Similarly, within the Greek culture, there were many 'pagan' religions, with Zeus, Artemis and others being worshipped. Yet these religions have since died out. In fact, of all the new religions that sprang up around Jesus' time, only one has survived: Christianity. This in itself says nothing about the resurrection. But it does indicate that the Jesus-movement had a strength and power to it that set it apart from anything else known at the time.

Shortly after the followers of Jesus started preaching about his resurrection, the Jewish authorities met to decide what to do with this new group and their teaching. The eventual decision was proposed by one of their leaders, Gamaliel, and backs up this point.

A Pharisee named Gamaliel, a teacher of the law, who was honoured by all the people, stood up in the Sanhedrin and ... addressed them: 'Men of Israel, consider carefully what you intend to do to these men. Some time ago Theudas appeared, claiming to be somebody, and about four hundred men rallied to him. He was killed, all his followers were dispersed, and it all came to nothing. After him, Judas the Galilean appeared in the days of the census and led a band of people in revolt. He too was killed, and all his followers were scattered. Therefore, in the present case I advise you: Leave these men alone! Let them go! For if their purpose or activity is of human origin, it will fail. But if it is from God, you will not be able to stop these men; you will only find yourselves fighting against God.'[22]

Nobody today has heard of Theudas or Judas the Galilean, but millions are followers of Jesus of Nazareth.

3. Christians today claim to know Jesus

It sounds strange, but the claim of millions of Christians today, from all around the world and from many different cultures, is that they know Jesus personally. The experience of a small handful of them are included in this book. They each claim that Jesus speaks to them, listens to them, comforts them, directs them and challenges them. Above all, they claim that they are not communicating with a dead person, but relating to a person who is alive and well, although they cannot see him. Some dismiss this talk as being on a par with a child's imaginary friend, but it is intelligent adults who make these claims, and they cannot be lightly dismissed. Christians will speak of their personal experience of Christ in a way that is compelling and cannot be denied. Would so many people claim such things if Jesus were still dead? We would have to conclude that they were all deluded and perhaps a little deranged.

Conclusion: a 'leap' of faith?

We have seen that all the evidence points towards the resurrection of Jesus really having happened: the alternative explanations of the empty tomb and sightings of Jesus have been found wanting, and the objections of scientists and philosophers have been seen to be unfounded. When it comes to assessing the claims of the disciples, historians and lawyers have given their firm support. As Sherlock Holmes said, 'When you have eliminated the impossible, whatever remains, however improbable, must be the truth.'

But where do we go from here?

A school pupil once defined faith as 'Believing what you know ain't true.' Similarly, many people seem to think it intellectual suicide to have faith, and imagine that to become a Christian involves a huge leap of faith. In reality, however, all of us have faith. If you are reading this book sitting down, you have faith in the manufacturer of the chair that it will support your weight and not collapse under you. It might seem like a very small amount of faith or risk is involved in sitting on the chair, but it is faith nonetheless. Likewise, whenever anyone walks across a bridge, they exercise faith in that bridge. Having seen lorries trundle over it without plunging into the river below, their faith is boosted that it can and will sustain their weight. As they put one foot in front of the other, they exercise trust in the bridge.

Imagine you are trekking in the mountains of Nepal when you come across a vast chasm with a flimsy-looking rope bridge strung between the two sides. Peering over the edge of the chasm, you see that it is hundreds of feet deep. There are no other bridges marked on the map, and certainly no way down the sides of the chasm. Would you cross it?

As you stand there pondering, some locals come up behind you, confidently step onto the bridge and make their way across successfully. Travellers come in the other direction, and again step onto the bridge without a moment's hesitation. The bridge bobs and sways but stays in one piece and doesn't throw people to their deaths.

Of course, it takes more faith to cross that rope bridge in Nepal than it does to cross a concrete bridge at home. Yet it takes less faith than before, having watched others cross the bridge success- fully. Taking a deep breath, you follow in the footsteps of others, and step out over the chasm. Your faith in the bridge is not suicidal, but reasonable.

When it comes to believing the resurrection, the intelligent inquirer discovers that given the historical supporting evidence, and the experience of others who've put their trust in the risen

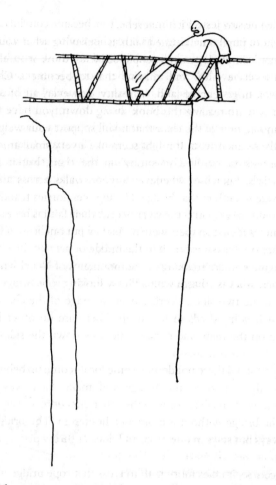

Jesus, what was once imagined as a massive jump to faith turns out to be no further than a small step. Believing in the resurrection is not intellectually suicidal, but reasonable. The question facing you is whether you will rely on the evidence to take that step.

I've already mentioned Thomas, the original arch-sceptic. He said he wouldn't believe Jesus had risen again unless he put his hands where the nails had been in Jesus' body. He was honest about his doubts and did not trust his friends who had seen Jesus alive again.

But when he saw Jesus for himself, he, too, became convinced. Jesus then said to him something which reaches out to us: 'Because you have seen me, you have believed; blessed are those who have not seen and yet have believed.'[23] In other words, Jesus promises that those who believe in him and his resurrection today are blessed.

It is like those who venture onto the rope bridge in the Himalayas: the views are breathtakingly spectacular, but they can only be seen from the bridge. As a Christian, I can say that knowing Jesus is absolutely wonderful – but to get that knowledge for yourself, you'll have to take a small step of faith and join me on the bridge.

Are you willing to take the first step, by believing that Jesus rose from the dead? To change the metaphor, there can be no sitting on the fence on this issue: it either did or did not happen. In a court of law, a juror cannot abstain from voting. You have heard the evidence; what is your verdict: is Jesus dead or alive?

real lives

Sir Lionel

Sir Lionel Luckhoo was a remarkable man. The hit cartoon 'The Simpsons' ironically even named one of its characters after him. The cartoon lawyer, Lionel Hutz, never won a case; by contrast, the real-life Sir Lionel achieved 245 consecutive murder acquittals, prompting 'The Guinness Book of Records' to hail him as the world's 'most successful' lawyer.[24] In addition, he was elected mayor four times; uniquely was appointed as High Commissioner for both Guyana and Barbados at the same time; and was twice knighted by the Queen.

It was only at the age of sixty-four that Sir Lionel became a believing Christian, but 'the transformation was immediate. From that day my life changed – I moved from death to life, from darkness to light . . . I found real peace and happiness and joy.'[25]

For Sir Lionel, Jesus' empty tomb set him apart from other religious leaders. 'Whereas the tomb of Mohammad in Medina holds the bones of Mohammad, and the tomb in Shantung holds the bones of Confucius and the tomb in Nepal holds the bones of Buddha . . . There are no bones in the tomb that once held Jesus, for he is risen.'[26]

What did 'the world's most successful lawyer' make of Jesus' resurrection? He once wrote, 'I have spent more than forty-two years as a defence trial lawyer appearing in many parts of the world and am still in active practice. I say unequivocally the evidence for the resurrection of Jesus Christ is so overwhelming that it compels acceptance by proof which leaves absolutely no room for doubt.'

But did he have any other evidence? Sir Lionel continued, 'I am often asked, how do you know Jesus lives? The answer I give is because Jesus is the risen Christ of the empty tomb, and . . . and this is most important, because he lives in my heart.'[27]

part three

So what?

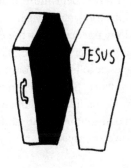 

What's Jesus' resurrection
got to do with me?

So what?

10 What are the implications of Jesus' resurrection?

What's Jesus' resurrection
got to do with me?

10. What are the implications of Jesus' resurrection?

'So what?' people ask. 'So one man rose from the dead two thousand years ago. What's the big deal?'

In this chapter, I want to show you that the fact that Jesus rose from the dead has serious implications for us. To tease out what those implications are, we're going to join a devoutly religious man called Saul travelling along Damascus Road with some friends a couple of years after Jesus' death. As he was travelling, he saw a blinding flash of light – and it wasn't a speed camera . . .

A sceptic's life-changing experience

Many years later, Saul (by then called Paul) was recounting his experience while on trial before a king.[1] Paul, a Jew, admitted that he *was* what might now be called a religious fundamentalist. But as so often in the Middle East even now, his zealousness was misplaced: he used violence to impose his religious views on other people. His particular targets were the first followers of Jesus. As he put it:

> ... I was convinced that I ought to do all that was possible to
> oppose the name of Jesus of Nazareth. And that is just what I did
> in Jerusalem. On the authority of the chief priests [the religious
> leaders] I put many of the saints [Christians] in prison, and when
> they were put to death, I cast my vote against them. Many a time
> I went from one synagogue to another to have them punished ...
> In my obsession against them, I even went to foreign cities to
> persecute them.

Not the nicest of people. And certainly not a believer in Jesus.

'On one of those journeys,' Paul continued, 'I was going to Damascus with the authority and commission of the chief priests. About noon ... as I was on the road, I saw a light from heaven, brighter than the sun, blazing around me and my companions. We all fell to the ground.' Paul 'heard a voice' saying to him, 'Saul, Saul, why do you persecute me?'

Unable to see and baffled as to who was speaking, Paul asked, 'Who are you, Lord?'

Then came the moment that must have felt like an earthquake in Paul's mind. The voice replied, 'I am Jesus.'

Imagine it: the same man that Paul had rubbished and opposed so intensely that he even travelled abroad simply to hound and wipe out his followers – this very person was now speaking to him! Paul couldn't deny his experience – apart from anything else, he was temporarily blinded. I can imagine Paul sitting in his darkness as the after-shocks of his experience rumbled through his mind.

Paul had thought Jesus was dead and buried, but he was forced to change his mind: Jesus was in fact well and truly alive. Paul had travelled the Damascus road to imprison Christians but by the time he arrived he was a changed man. Three days later, Paul became a Christian, and was to become one of the most influential Christians in history.

> **Paul had thought Jesus was dead and buried, but he was forced to change his mind.**

Implications about Jesus
Paul also became a prolific letter-writer, leaving us a clear record of some of the crucial new conclusions he came to about Jesus.

Who Jesus is
In chapter 1 I said that Jesus' resurrection was the final proof of his outrageous claim to be God in human flesh. Such an assertion has always provoked attacks, the most recent of which has come via Dan Brown's *The Da Vinci Code*. Brown makes out that Jesus' divinity was an idea first proposed almost three hundred years after Jesus' death, and that even then church leaders accepted it on a 'relatively close vote'.[2]

In fact, nothing could be further from the truth. There are historical documents from the first century onwards that clearly indicate a belief that Jesus was divine. Even the Roman governor Pliny (who dismissed Christianity as a foolish superstition) recorded in AD 112 that 'Christians ... were accustomed to meet and sing ... to Christ as to a god.'[3] The belief that Jesus was God in human flesh was so widespread that when international church leaders gathered in AD 325, the vote in support of Jesus' divinity was extremely clear-cut: out of well over two hundred bishops present, only two demurred. Not even the most optimistic spin doctor could call that 'a close vote'!

Some of the very earliest documents describing Jesus as God are those written by Paul himself. In one letter, he described Jesus as 'the image of the invisible God.' A friend of mine is living abroad for a year at the moment, but a picture of her is on my desk. That's an image of my invisible (but definitely not imaginary) friend. How much better to have the living, breathing Jesus as an image of the living God! Paul went on to assert that 'in Christ all the fullness of the Deity lives in bodily form.'[4] Elsewhere he talks about 'our great God and Saviour, Jesus Christ.'[5]

Many other examples from Paul's writings could be given, but the point is this: when he met the risen Jesus, Paul was forced to realize that Jesus wasn't the evil man he once thought. Rather, he was, and is, God himself.

What's your view of Jesus at the moment? Is it changing as you read this book?

Jesus is alive today

At the risk of stating the obvious, another of the implications of Jesus' resurrection is that he's still alive today. When Jesus raised other people from the dead, those were technically 'resuscitations' – people came back to life, but their new life wasn't permanent. They died again. However, when Paul and the other Christian leaders talked about Jesus, they were clear that his was a 'resurrection': a permanent state of life, having conquered death completely. After forty days of people meeting the risen Jesus on earth, he was taken up to heaven before his friends' eyes,[6] but they were absolutely clear that he hadn't died a second time.

Paul's own dramatic experience convinced him that Jesus is alive. He clearly pictures Jesus as God's right-hand man in heaven,[7] worthy of our worship and allegiance. For Paul, there was no sense in which Jesus was 'out of sight and out of mind'. On the contrary, because Jesus was sitting at the position of all power and authority in the universe, he was very much in Paul's mind at all times. For example, he talks of speaking to Jesus and hearing him speak, of living to please Jesus, and of Jesus' continued activity through his church.

Christians today say the same things. They do not follow a dead man; they worship the risen Jesus. He may be out of sight, but he's very much alive.

> **Christians do not follow a dead man;**
> **they worship the risen Jesus.**

How does it make you feel to think of Jesus as alive, and watching over our lives?

Jesus will come back one day
To Paul's changed mindset, Jesus' resurrection and continued life in heaven were closely aligned with a strong belief that Jesus would come again. In the West, we tend to think that our world will carry on without end – unless some global nuclear disaster occurs or some worldwide climate change happens which renders human life impossible. Jesus spoke differently. He clearly thought that human history would have an end – precipitated by his return.

Jesus spoke about his return in very vivid language, to underline its universal significance: 'But in those days ... "The sun will be darkened and the moon will not give its light; the stars will fall from the sky, and the heavenly bodies will be shaken." At that time, people will see the Son of Man [Jesus' title for himself] coming in clouds with great power and glory.'[8] Likewise, his disciples were told that 'This same Jesus, who has been taken from you into heaven, will come back in the same way you have seen him go into heaven.'[9]

It's not surprising, then, that Paul himself quickly realized that another implication of Jesus' resurrection was that he would one day return. He wrote, 'we eagerly await a saviour from there [heaven], the Lord Jesus Christ.'[10] Many people scoff at the idea that Jesus will one day come back to this earth, to bring history to its climax and this world as we know it to a culmination. But Jesus predicted many things in the course of his life which did come true. In fact, his own second coming is the only prophecy he made which has yet to be completed.

> **Jesus predicted many things in the course of his life which did come true. In fact, his own second coming is the only prophecy he made which has yet to be completed.**

But what will happen when Jesus returns?

- *We will face Jesus as our judge.* Maybe one of the reasons many people dismiss the idea of Jesus' return is that they don't like the idea which goes with it: that we will face Jesus as our judge. Reading the gospels, it's very striking that Jesus takes it for granted that he will be our judge when we see him face to face on his return.[11] Jesus reassures us that his judgment won't be in any way unfair, 'for I seek not to please myself but him who sent me.'[12] For Paul, Jesus' judgment was another implication of his resurrection. Speaking to philosophers in Athens, he described how God 'has set a day when he will judge the world with justice by the man he has appointed. He has given proof of this to all people by raising him [Jesus] from the dead.'[13]

- *A separation will take place.* In one of Jesus' parables, he makes it clear that a separation will take place when he judges: 'When the Son of Man comes ... all the nations will be gathered before him, and he will separate the people one from another as a shepherd separates the sheep from the goats. He will put the sheep on his right and the goats on his left.'[14] In part 1, we looked at the two destinies that he talked about: heaven and hell. Paul's own teaching about life after death was radically influenced by Jesus' resurrection.[15] Like him, Paul now believed that a separation would take place,[16] with two possible destinies: an unimaginably glorious heaven[17] and an horrendously awful hell.[18]

So how will Jesus make his judgment? Jesus said that his judgment and separation will be based on our response to him and his teaching: 'If anyone is ashamed of me and my words in this . . . generation, the Son of Man will be ashamed of him when he comes.'[19] In other words, Jesus' verdict on us then will be directly related to our verdict on him now: if we're ashamed of him now, not wanting to know him, then he'll be ashamed of us then, not wanting to know us.

Before Paul's life-changing experience, the suggestions that Jesus would be our judge and that his judgment would be based on our response to him would have been unthinkable. But having realized that Jesus was God in human flesh who would return as our judge, it became yet another implication of Jesus' resurrection. Paul clearly taught that God will reject and punish those who reject him, and accept those who accept him.[20]

Such teaching has massive implications for us: we would be very well advised to accept Jesus! Although many people react with horror to the thought of God rejecting anybody (claiming that it makes him out to be sadistic), this basis for judgment turns out to be little more than common courtesy. For example, if a friend or colleague snubs you publicly one day, they couldn't really expect you to help them out of a tight spot the next – at least, not without at first apologizing. Similarly, we shouldn't expect Jesus to accept us if we've spent all of our lives ignoring him!

In this section, we've seen how Paul's views about Jesus changed completely after his life-changing experience. It's hard to imagine a greater change in perception: beforehand, Paul had thought of Jesus as an evil man who'd deserved his awful death under God's judgment. Afterwards, Paul realized that Jesus had indeed risen from the dead, was God in human flesh, and was alive and reigning in heaven. Previously, Paul had judged Jesus. Now he realized that one day Jesus would return and judge him on the basis of his own response to Jesus. It had become obvious for Paul that Jesus' resurrection didn't just have *theoretical* implications about Jesus; it had *personal* implications for him as well. Jesus' resurrection affected Paul's eternal destiny.

> **If Jesus rose from the dead, Christianity is shown to be something infinitely more important than a simple 'take it or leave it' lifestyle choice.**

Of course, what Paul had realized wasn't just true for him: it's true for all of us. If Jesus rose from the dead, Christianity is shown to be something infinitely more important than a simple 'take it or leave it' lifestyle choice. If Jesus rose from the dead, he is God over us, alive and reigning in heaven, one day to return and judge us on the basis of our response to him. That statement should be enough to make all of us sit up and take notice! But that's only the first part of our answer to the 'So what?' question. Paul discovered that there are still more implications stemming from Jesus' resurrection.

Implications about us

When I was a teenager, I remember my parents sitting down with me one mealtime and telling me that Dad was leaving his job. For a few minutes, that was fine. But as the discussion went on, it became clear that we might have to move for Dad to get a new job. All of a sudden, the knock-on effects of my dad leaving his job became all too apparent: I might have to move away from my friends, and from the band that I so loved playing in. I was devastated.

When Paul met the risen Jesus, I suspect he was equally devastated when he began to figure out the knock-on effects of what he now knew to be true about Jesus himself.

The way to know God is through Jesus

Paul had always realized that God created us to *know* him, and that we humans are prone to take him for granted or turn away from him. For example, when recounting the history of his people (the Jews), he wrote that 'Although they knew God, they neither glorified him as God nor gave thanks to him' and that 'they did not think it worthwhile to retain the knowledge of God.'[21]

But when Paul understood that God had supremely revealed himself in Jesus, he suddenly realized that the way to know God now was through Jesus. Jesus himself had said as much. He defined 'eternal life' not in terms of a *quantity* of life, but a *quality* of relationship: 'This is eternal life: that they may *know* you, the only true God, and Jesus Christ, whom you have sent.'[22] It comes as no surprise then, that after becoming a Christian, Paul could talk about the 'surpassing greatness of knowing Christ Jesus my Lord.'[23]

Indeed, Jesus had said that the *only* way to know God was through him: 'I am the way and the truth and the life. No-one comes to the Father except through me.'[24] Paul came to realize that truth as well: 'There is only one God, and Christ Jesus is the only one who can bring us to God.'[25]

The implication for us, then, is that if we want to know God, we can do so only through Jesus.

By nature, we are separated from God

Most of us think that we're pretty decent people. We generally abide by the laws of the land (at least, we don't do anything that will harm other people); we work fairly hard to earn our wage, then pay our taxes and even give some money to charity; our friends like us; we do our best to be nice to people we find awkward. In our minds, we take that a step further: we suppose that because *we* think fairly highly of ourselves, so does *God*. Those of us with any religious background presume that counts in our favour as well.

Paul thought in exactly that kind of way before his life-changing encounter. Without a hint of modesty he wrote, 'Others may brag about themselves, but I have more reason to brag than anyone else'! In fact, he would have looked down on most of us for passively assuming that God likes us. By contrast, his proactive aim in life was to please God. What's more, he thought he had the best possible pedigree to be in God's good books and claimed, 'I did everything the Law demands in order to please God.'

But once again, Jesus resurrection' and its implications changed his entire mindset. His letter continues, 'But Christ has shown me that what I once thought was valuable is worthless . . . I could not make myself acceptable to God by obeying the Law.'[26] For someone whose whole life revolved around trying to please God, that was his worst nightmare! The foundation of his life's work had been blown apart, and everything he'd strived so hard to achieve collapsed in a miserable heap.

Specifically, Paul realized that pleasing God now entailed

pleasing Jesus – which was exactly the opposite of what he'd been doing previously, as he went round attacking Jesus' followers! It's not surprising that years later he described himself as 'the worst of sinners.'[27]

'Sin' is a word often used by Christians, but what exactly does it mean? Most people think of sin as something 'naughty but nice' – an act that we instinctively know is wrong, but is so pleasurable that we'll do it anyway. But when Jesus talks about sin, his understanding is quite different. At its root, he says that people are sinful 'because people do not believe in me.'[28] So sin isn't first and foremost breaking one of God's moral *rules* by pretending they don't exist. Sin is breaking God's *heart* by ignoring him. If we really believed in Jesus, we'd understand that his moral rules are put there for our *benefit* (in much the same way as a mother tells her child not to play near the cooker), and we'd then seek to live by them. When we don't seek to live by them, it's a sure sign that we don't really believe in Jesus.

Someone once said that 'The heart of the human problem is the problem of the human heart.' Jesus would agree, because when our hearts don't truly believe in him, the consequence is that we ignore the pattern for living that he's given us. As he put it, 'What comes from your heart is what makes you unclean. Out of your heart come evil thoughts, vulgar deeds, stealing, murder, unfaithfulness in marriage, greed, meanness, deceit, indecency, envy,

insults, pride, and foolishness.' Not surprisingly, the result of such rebellion against God in both attitude and action is that we're estranged from him: 'All of these come from your heart, and they are what make you unfit to worship God.'[29]

So our sin separates us from God, and the punishment for sin is death.[30] Again, that sounds harsh at first, but just as committing treason against one's nation by betraying your homeland deserves to result in punishment from the state authorities, so committing treason against God by rejecting his rightful authority over our lives deservedly results in divine punishment. Paul knew that unless apology was made and pardon granted, all sin would be punished: we would remain separated from God even beyond death.[31]

We are spiritually dead

I've already noted that our society is undergoing a resurgence of interest in 'spirituality'. Go into any bookstore and the section marked 'Religion and Spirituality' is bursting off the shelves; 'Mind, Body and Spirit' exhibitions are becoming a rapidly growing industry. There seem to be hundreds of options, and almost as many opinions. But if there is a God who makes himself known the key question isn't 'What do *we* make of these spiritualities?' but 'What does *God* make of them?'

The answer to that question is startling, but flows on from the conclusion of the previous section – that we are separated from God. Just as Paul used to think of himself as living a life that was pleasing to God, so he thought himself very well connected to God. But having realized that, in fact, he was opposing and hurting God, his new conclusion on his previous spiritual state was dramatic: he was spiritually dead. As he put it years later when writing to Christians, 'In the past, you were dead because you sinned and fought against God.'[32]

It sounds very bleak to say that we're spiritually dead – especially when some people have what they describe as 'spiritual experiences'. But although such experiences may move people deeply, we need to know whether they genuinely connect people with God, or are purely psychological in their effect. For all the spiritual experiences Paul had felt before he became a follower of Jesus (through personal prayer, private meditation and public religious ceremonies, etc.), he now realized that they'd had absolutely *no* effect on his relationship with God. He'd been spiritually dead.

Once again, Paul's new conclusion reflects what Jesus himself had taught. Speaking to someone who considered himself very spiritual, Jesus told him that 'no-one can see the kingdom of God unless they are born again'. Jesus went on to make it clear that he wasn't suggesting that people be *physically* born again – that would be impossible. What was necessary was that everyone was 'born of the Spirit'[33] – in other words, that they have a spiritual rebirth, or to be more precise, a spiritual birth.

Jesus was clear, and Paul now agreed with him: if someone hasn't been spiritually born, they're not yet spiritually alive, and therefore as good as dead!

How does that verdict make you feel?

A seismic experience

When telling the story of Paul's encounter with Jesus, I described the moment of his realization that Jesus was alive as being like an earthquake in Paul's mind. The obvious effect of an earthquake is that buildings collapse, but they can be rebuilt with time. But many earthquakes leave more subtle effects that are only noticed later: the whole lie of the land changes. Rivers change their course. New hills or lakes appear. Such changes are permanent.

Paul's life-changing meeting with the risen Jesus had a series of very obvious effects:

- he realized that Jesus wasn't an evil man but God in human flesh;
- he realized that Jesus wasn't dead in his grave, but alive and reigning in heaven;

- he realized his judgment of Jesus had been completely wrong and inappropriate. One day Jesus would return to earth, and judge him on his response to Jesus.

But the whole lie of the land in Paul's mind changed permanently as well:

- he realized that the way to know God was through Jesus, not through obeying rules;
- he realized that his previous attempts at pleasing God were useless, and that far from being near perfect, he was in fact the worst of sinners;
- he realized that he was spiritually dead.

These implications of Jesus' resurrection are incredibly profound and far-reaching – not just for Paul, but for each one of us. That Jesus was raised from the dead turns out to have an effect on our eternal destinies! But it also tells us a lot about our lives now and how we can get to know God.

Of course, it feels awful to be declared 'spiritually dead'. But Paul's experience should, in fact, give us great optimism. After all, when he encountered the risen Jesus, he wasn't subjected to revenge and judgment. Far from it. He experienced a love so deep that he was forgiven, and his life was turned around. As he put it, 'Even though I was once a blasphemer and a persecutor and a violent man, I was shown mercy because I acted in ignorance and unbelief. The grace of our Lord was poured out on me abundantly, along with the faith and love that are in Christ Jesus.'[34] He stopped attacking Christians and started encouraging people to become Christians; he quit trying to close churches and began to found them instead.

Paul's seismic experience was doubtless very painful for him – emotionally as well as physically. But it turned out to be for his good. He couldn't be 'born again' until he'd acknowledged he was spiritually dead. But having realized his terrible mistake, he received Jesus' gift of new life. He was no longer dead but alive: 'We were dead because of our sins, but God loved us so much that he made us alive with Christ.'[35]

But how exactly can Jesus make us alive? To answer that question, we need to wind the clock back thirty-six hours from Easter Sunday morning to Good Friday afternoon.

Tony works for churches in Nottinghamshire, and until recently was chaplain to Manchester City Football Club.

Tony, what do you make of Jesus?

Sport was my god, so when a serious hockey accident on my twentieth birthday meant that sport in the future was doubtful, an encouragement to read about Jesus in the gospels was an offer I couldn't refuse.

I read John 8.1–11, and was stunned. For a start, the story seemed real. Before, my impression of the Bible was of a fairy tale, not at all related to real life. I found in this passage a 'woman taken in adultery', who had been set up by religious hypocrites. I discovered that Jesus could deal with the hypocrites, but could also bring direction and healing to a broken, humiliated woman.

I read the trial of Jesus. When asked (Mark 14.61–62), 'Are you the Christ, the Son of the Blessed One?' he replied, 'I am.' For one who was to train to be a barrister after university, even I could work out there could only be one of three conclusions to this claim. He was either bad, mad or telling the truth. Nothing I read in the gospels suggested Jesus was bad or mad, so I had to pursue the possibility that he was telling the truth, claiming to be the Son of God.

I read Luke 23.39–43. I understood why one of the thieves was cursing him, but it was the other thief that fascinated me. Dying slowly and painfully, Jesus assured the thief that he would join him in paradise; only the Son of God could possibly have that authority, but I recognized that Jesus had to die for it to be possible.

I was blown away by Jesus; he was not what I expected, but I had to face the fact that if he was the Son of God, my allegiance to him was non-negotiable. He's now been my Lord and Saviour for over thirty years, with not an ounce of regret.

real lives

Miguel

Miguel worked for seventeen years as a fishing/marine engineer in Brazil. Nine years ago he helped start a new church; it now has over one thousand members.

Miguel, what do you make of Jesus?

As a young adult, I never went to church and considered religion unnecessary for being a good citizen. I played basketball, and spent much time travelling the Brazilian coastline looking for waves and anything connected with the surf culture.

Entering university, I decided to study Marine/Fish Engineering. At university I met up again with many friends, and some of them seemed to have something different about them: they spoke of Christ, and their lives had changed. It had quite an impact and attracted me greatly, especially the fact that they seemed to really 'live'.

I began going to a Christian group and became interested in Jesus' words, so I began to read the Bible. I read the whole of the New Testament and I was mesmerized by the stories, and by Jesus Christ. I was amazed by his power over everything from disease to the weather. And whoever he met – those suffering injustice, the hopeless, the sick, the lost, children – he always had a face of love.

One day, I was invited to a prayer gathering for young people, and there, in the middle of a prayer, I felt the presence of Jesus Christ more alive than anything, and I was scared to open my eyes for fear of seeing Christ himself in that room. A young man spoke some prophetic words which addressed me directly, speaking about my life and my anxieties.

I handed my life over to Jesus there and then, and asked him to give me the strength to live my life for him. Something happened inside me, a certain conviction that Jesus was alive and with me in that place, a conviction that continues today, every waking moment of my life.

Jesus, alive and present, has been the absolute certainty of my life.

11. Life from death

I wonder what your instinctive reaction is when you see an image of Jesus' death? They crop up everywhere – on church buildings, as jewellery, in art. Many people tend not to give the image a second thought. To them, the cross is a recognizable marketing symbol, but that's about as far as it goes. That's understandable when the depiction is of an empty cross, or shows Jesus hanging serenely. But in reality, the cross was a place of grisly execution. We would be shocked, probably disgusted, if someone were to wear jewellery

that showed an electric chair or syringe loaded with a lethal injection – but that's the shock we should feel on seeing a cross.

Of course, religious art and cinematic portrayals of Jesus' death sometimes begin to bring out the horror of the crucifixion. We can be sure that Jesus' face would have been racked with a pain greater than most of us will ever know. When we see these more realistic portrayals of Jesus' death, our reaction tends to be one of pity ('poor man, dying so young') or moral revulsion ('how barbaric of his executioners to inflict such a tortured death').

In the previous chapter, we looked at how Paul's understanding of Jesus and himself had changed in the light of his encounter with the risen Jesus. In this chapter, I want to explore one final implication of Paul's momentous experience: how his thinking about Jesus' death altered.

Why did Jesus die?

Most of us would be aghast to find someone cheering at the sight of Jesus' death. Paul, however, used to be just such a man. Although he wasn't present at the event, we can be sure he would have approved of Jesus' death with a look of smug satisfaction. It was people from the same religious sect as Paul who'd worked so hard to ensure that Jesus was crucified, and although he only rose to prominence in the sect a few years after Jesus' death, Paul quickly followed on where his predecessors had left off – this time, arranging for Jesus' followers to be executed.[1]

The wrong answer

Paul's approval of Jesus' death was on the grounds that Jesus had been a 'blasphemer' – someone who claimed to be God when in fact he wasn't. To Paul's intensely religious mind, that was the worst crime imaginable – and worthy of immediate death.[2] In addition, Paul believed that God had said, 'Cursed is everyone who is hung on a tree', so the fact that Jesus died on a wooden cross (rather than, for example, by stoning) simply confirmed Paul's view that Jesus was an evil man suffering God's judgment as he died.[3]

In short, Paul was delighted that Jesus died (and didn't mind in the slightest that it was such a painful death) because he believed that Jesus deserved to die. However, when Paul came to realize that Jesus was, in fact, alive again, his opinion of Jesus' death as God's deserved judgment was shattered.

The film *In the Name of the Father* recounted the story of the 'Guildford Four' – four men who were wrongly convicted of being involved in an IRA bombing. After fifteen years in prison their verdicts were overturned and they were released. The Prime Minister has since given a public apology for the miscarriage of justice they suffered.

The historical accounts of Jesus' trial leave no doubt that Jesus was innocent.

The Guildford Four's release from jail was proof that they'd now been declared innocent of the crime for which they were imprisoned. Similarly, when Jesus was released from the grave, it was the most stunning overturning of a sentence imaginable – and indicated beyond doubt that God declared him to be innocent of the crime for which he was executed.

In fact, the historical accounts of Jesus' trial leave no doubt that Jesus was innocent.[4] The religious authorities wanted him to be guilty, but had to rustle up false witnesses; his two judges found him innocent; the crowd only called for his death because they'd been stirred up by the religious leaders; even the Roman centurion in charge of the execution squad and one of the other men crucified with Jesus thought him innocent! Pilate, known as a ruthless ruler, found 'no basis for a charge' against Jesus, and only succumbed to the stubborn request for the death penalty because he was swayed by peer pressure.

Elsewhere, the Bible underlines Jesus' blamelessness, not just of the charges presented against him in his trials, but innocent of *all* wrongdoing. Before Jesus began his public ministry, he faced a series of temptations, none of which he gave in to. Jesus himself stressed that he was obedient to his heavenly Father. One Christian writer said that Jesus 'has been tempted in every way, just as we are – yet was without sin', describing him as 'holy, blameless, pure, set apart from sinners'. Paul called Jesus 'him who had no sin.'[5]

So Paul came to realize that Jesus didn't die because he was guilty. Rather, his resurrection indicated the exact opposite: that Jesus was completely innocent. Unique among the human race, he never rebelled against God or his laws (despite facing all the temptations we face), and so did not deserve to die. Yet the one perfectly innocent man who ever lived took the ultimate punishment: he was executed by one of the cruellest forms of death ever invented by the warped imagination of human beings.

Paul was left with a mystery that has puzzled many people since: why did God let Jesus die? Or to put it more bluntly: why did God himself die? Paul knew that God wouldn't have *let* Jesus die if he hadn't *intended* it to happen – but how could Jesus' death possibly be interpreted positively?

An inadequate answer
One common answer to that question through the years has been that Jesus died as an example of sacrificial love, in order to encourage us to be more loving towards each other. But that answer by itself is inadequate. An illustration will help explain why.

Suppose I take my wife for a romantic weekend in Paris, and we climb the Eiffel Tower to admire the views. Then suppose that I turn to my wife and say, 'I want to show you how much I love you', and with that I jump off the Tower, and plunge to my death. It wouldn't be a sign of love, would it? It would be a sign of madness! A death by itself doesn't demonstrate love.

But of course, a death *can* demonstrate love – immense love – if the person dies while protecting or rescuing someone else. Imagine if rather than going up the Eiffel Tower, my wife and I were to go for a moonlit stroll along the River Seine. If, while gazing adoringly into my eyes, she accidentally falls in the river and starts to struggle in the water, and if I manfully rescue her but drown in the process – well that *would* be demonstrating love, because I would have saved her. She would have benefited from my death.

A death can demonstrate love — immense love — if the person dies while protecting or rescuing someone else.

Paul certainly agreed that Jesus' death was a sign of love,[6] but realized that for it to be loving, someone else must benefit from his death. Jesus had sacrificed himself, but for whom?

A more complete answer
The startling conclusion that Paul came to was that Jesus 'Christ died *for us*'[7] and again, that 'he died *for all*.'[8] Paul came to realize that Jesus had sacrificed himself for Paul, and indeed for everyone, including you and me. Once again, it should be immediately obvious that Jesus' resurrection has implications that stretch across the centuries and touch each one of us personally.

Paul's conclusion was almost certainly reached having heard from others what Jesus himself had taught; for Jesus alluded to his death in some of his most famous sayings. Having described himself as the 'Good Shepherd', he made it clear that he wasn't talking about watching cute, fluffy lambs all day. Rather, he was going to 'lay down my life *for the sheep*.'[9] On another occasion, Jesus gave a definition of love that is often used on Remembrance Day, saying, 'Greater love has no-one than this: that he lay down his life *for his friends*.'[10] In Jesus' definition, that didn't refer to those who died in war, but to Jesus himself. On still another occasion, he said that he'd come to 'give his life as a ransom *for many*.'[11] When Jesus died, it was a demonstration of his immense love *for us*.

> Good Friday should be called 'Bad Friday' if it merely marked the pointless cutting short of a great life.

Good Friday should be called 'Bad Friday' if it merely marked the pointless cutting short of a great life. That we call it 'Good Friday' is because we can benefit from Jesus' death. Jesus knew, and Paul came to realize, what many people don't understand: that Jesus' death wasn't a tragedy, but would achieve something incredibly precious for us. But how exactly do we benefit from it?

The full answer

Here we come to the very core of Paul's new understanding of why Jesus died. Remember, Paul used to think of Jesus' death as a sign of God's judgment on a guilty man. Once he had appreciated that Jesus was anything but guilty, Paul was forced to re-evaluate his understanding of what was happening at the cross. He realized that Jesus' death was an act of God's love, for his own benefit as well as for everyone else. In addition to all this, at the back of Paul's mind was the burning problem that we highlighted in the previous chapter: that Paul was 'a sinner' – out of sorts with God – and he knew that his sin must be punished. As Paul considered these things, there was one delightful fact as well: when Jesus appeared to him, we might have expected Jesus to strike him down, considering what he'd done to Jesus' followers. Instead, Jesus had apparently accepted Paul into his service!

When Paul added all these various elements together, the conclusion he came to, and subsequently preached to thousands, was that 'Christ died *for our sins*.'[12] What was happening as Jesus died was a momentous exchange: Jesus was receiving the punishment for our offences against God. As Paul put it, 'Christ never sinned! But God treated him as a sinner.'[13] We saw in the previous chapter that Paul understood our rejection of God to be incredibly serious and only forgivable at a cost. In past times, that cost had been the sacrifice of the lives of many innocent animals. But after meeting Jesus, Paul realized that the old system of sacrifices had been superseded and done away with by one final, perfect sacrifice – of Jesus himself. Paul wrote, 'God . . . sent his own Son to be like us sinners and to be a sacrifice for our sin.'[14]

So Jesus took our guilt and punishment from us. But what was the other part of this exchange? Amazingly, it's that we're treated as Jesus should have been: we're declared innocent and put right with God, free from all punishment. Our guilty past is wiped out, enabling our friendship with God to be resumed. As Paul wrote, 'God was reconciling the world to himself in Christ, not counting people's sins against them.'[15]

Once more, Paul's conclusion wasn't original, and was almost certainly founded on the teaching of Jesus. When he'd shared his last meal with his closest followers, shortly before he was arrested and convicted, Jesus had explained what was going to happen. In a deeply symbolic gesture, he'd taken bread and wine, and likened them to his own body and blood. He said his body was going to be broken, and his blood 'poured out for many for the forgiveness of sins.'[16] Hours later, symbolism became reality on the cross.

Do you remember the swaps we used to make in playground card-collection games: 'I'll give you this card (that you really, really want in your collection) in exchange for those five cards (that you don't need, and I wouldn't mind having)'? What Jesus was achieving as he died was an exchange of the most enormous proportions.

Here, then, is the heart of the Christian faith. As Paul thought of Jesus dying on the cross, his former sense of smug jubilation was shown up not only as grossly misplaced, but also part of the very reason Jesus had died. In dying, Jesus had taken on himself the punishment for Paul's offences – so that Paul's friendship with God, both before and after death, could be restored. We can only imagine the flood of emotions Paul felt as he first truly understood why Jesus had died. Later on, he could barely contain himself, writing, 'Thanks be to God for his indescribable gift!'[17]

But Paul also knew that he wasn't the only beneficiary of Jesus' death. The way his own life had been turned around by Jesus' death and resurrection was proof that anyone's life – maybe even yours – could be similarly changed. As he put it, 'Since I was worse than anyone else, God had mercy on me ... so that others would put their faith in Christ and have eternal life.'[18]

In the previous chapter, we saw that ignoring God and rejecting his rules separates us from him and makes us spiritually dead. In this chapter, we've seen that Jesus died for all, to blot out those past offences and give us the possibility of renewed spiritual life – life in friendship with God. Do you long for your past offences to be wiped out, and guilt taken away? Deep down, do you wish you could find unconditional and unwavering acceptance and friendship? Paul found those when he realized why Jesus had died. Paul was made spiritually alive.

Jesus' death: the moment of new life

On a family holiday in the USA when I was growing up, we visited Yellowstone National Park. It's a vast and spectacular area; none more so than in the summer of our visit, when forest fires damaged huge swathes of land. To a young boy, the fires were rather exciting: I can remember leaning out of our car window with a video camera, filming fire-filled forest on either side of the road. My parents took the park rangers' screamed instructions slightly more seriously: put your foot on the gas and get out as quickly as you can. The entrance to the park was closed as soon as we left.

To the average tourist, the fires were a tragedy. Not only were holiday plans marred, but thousands of trees were destroyed and hundreds of animals were killed. However, those who knew the park well were somewhat less disappointed. Forest fires are a natural part of the life of such ecosystems, and fires of that scale probably occur every two hundred years or so. Visitors the following year didn't just see blackened trees, but at the foot of those trees, spectacular displays of fresh wildflower growth feeding on fallen ash. Perhaps even more remarkably, the predominant pine trees of the forest only release their seeds under considerable heat – the sort of heat generated by a fire. So even as the old trees were being scorched, they were releasing the seeds of new life. Today, the landscape is no longer dominated by the old, dead trees, but by a vast number of healthy young trees – trees that could only be planted because of the fire.

We've been exploring the question of why Jesus died. As with those forest fires, his death was not the tragedy that it seemed. It was, in fact, the moment when the seeds of new life were released – indeed, the *only* way new life could start. As he died, Jesus made it possible for us to be 'born again', to become spiritually alive – reconnected with God.

Jesus himself knew that his death would be the culmination of his life's work and the moment of new birth. Often, Jesus' teaching was deliberately obtuse, designed to get people thinking. But when talking about his death, his message was loud and clear. He told his friends that he 'must suffer many things and be rejected by the elders, chief priests and teachers of the law, and . . . must be killed.' His warning that his future would be full of suffering was particularly insistent.[19] For him, this future wasn't optional. He *must* suffer and *must* be killed.

Jesus held on to that conviction even as he hung on the cross. As he died, Jesus shouted out, 'It is finished!'[20] In Jesus' day, that phrase was used much as we use the phrase 'Paid in full' to declare a debt cleared. In other words, it's a shout of triumph not failure – just like someone might celebrate today when they've finally paid off their student loan or mortgage. It's significant that Jesus didn't cry in defeat as he died, and reserve this shout of triumph for his resurrection morning. He knew that as he died, he was paying in full for the sins of the world. His resurrection was merely the vindication that his sacrifice had been acceptable to God.

One of the most moving pieces of poetry in the entire Bible was written hundreds of years before Jesus' death, yet provides us with a wonderfully clear explanation of what it achieved.

But the fact is, it was *our* pains he carried –
our disfigurements, all the things wrong with us.
We thought he brought it on himself,
that God was punishing him for his own failures.
But it was our sins that did that to him,
that ripped and tore and crushed him – *our* sins!
He took the punishment, and that made us whole.

Through his bruises we get healed.
We're all like sheep who've wandered off and got lost.
We've all done our own thing, gone our own way.
And God has piled all our sins, everything we've done wrong,
on him, on him.[21]

When Jesus' followers re-read this poem after Jesus' death and resurrection, they understood that it was about him, and began to tell everyone they could the good news: anyone who trusted that Jesus had taken the punishment for their sins when he died would be pardoned for their offences and guaranteed eternal life.

Faith in Jesus' death: the means of new life
Jesus' followers told this good news to as many people as they could. 'Everyone who believes in him receives forgiveness of sins through his name.' 'Believe in the Lord Jesus, and you will be saved.'[22] They told others this news, because they knew it was true for themselves. Paul's touching personal confession of faith can be echoed by any Christian: 'the Son of God ... loved *me*, and gave himself for *me*.'[23]

**God offers us a free gift —
but we have to 'apply' for it.**

One final point must be made as we close this chapter, and it's highlighted in those quotes just given. Although God's offer of forgiveness is available to everyone, it's not credited to us automatically. A few years ago, my building society was floated on the stock exchange. All their existing customers could apply for shares that wouldn't cost anything to buy, but could be sold on at 100% profit. It was as close as you could get to 'free money' – but you had to apply. Similarly, God offers us a free gift – but we have to 'apply' for it.

The 'application process' is ludicrously simple: all one has to do is 'believe in the Lord Jesus'. In the previous chapter, we saw how Paul realized that all his concerted efforts to get into God's good books were declared useless by Jesus' resurrection and its implications. As he put it, 'I could not make myself acceptable to God by obeying the Law.' Now he understood that 'God accepted me simply because of my faith [i.e. belief] in Christ.'[24]

In fact, such a message isn't just ludicrously simple, it's offensively simple, because it strips us of any ability to contribute towards our rescue. For Paul, as for those of us who like to think of ourselves as essentially good people, that is very humbling. But it is also wonderfully liberating, for if we had to work to be forgiven by God, we'd never think we'd done enough to earn it. Neither would we have any assurance that our offences had been wiped out. Believing in Jesus' death as the sole grounds of our rescue enables us to look back to the cross with absolute confidence that God now accepts us.

The most famous verse in the Bible underlines this point. Speaking in advance about the results of his own death, Jesus said, 'For God so loved the world that he gave his one and only Son, that whoever believes in him shall not perish but have eternal life.'[25] Later, he said, 'I tell you the truth, whoever hears my word and believes him who sent me has eternal life and will not be condemned; he has crossed over from death to life.'[26] However, there's a flip-side to that promise: 'Whoever does not believe stands condemned already because he has not believed in the name of God's one and only Son.'[27]

In this chapter, we've discovered how Paul was, and how we can be, 'made alive with Christ': through trusting in the fact of Jesus' sacrificial death. We can contribute nothing, for Jesus has already paid in full: 'We were dead because of our sins, but God loved us so much that he made us alive with Christ, and God's wonderful kindness is what saves you.' Incredibly, Paul then equates what happens to those who believe with what happened to Jesus: 'God raised us from death to life with Christ Jesus, and he has given us a place beside Christ in heaven.'[28]

As we've unpacked the implications of Jesus' resurrection, it's become clear that the real question is no longer 'Is *Jesus* dead or alive?' It's now this: 'Are *you* dead or alive?'

real lives

Ian is currently studying towards a PhD at the University of Cambridge.

Ian

Ian, why is Jesus' death so important to you?

When I left home, I took a gap year working in industry. During that year, I started asking questions about the purpose of life. It just didn't seem to make any sense or have any point. Despite having a 'bright future' ahead of me, I became severely depressed and thought my life worthless.

As I tried to make sense of my life I reasoned that God must be out there, so I started reading the Bible to try to find some answers. When I got to university, I met some students who invited me to the Christian Union. I thought I was a Christian because I believed Jesus was God but I soon realized I was wrong. At one of the first meetings I saw for the first time that Jesus came to earth to die for me on the cross. He died to take the punishment that I deserve in living for myself and not for God.

When I realized this I was awestruck. I had thought my life was absolutely worthless but Jesus obviously thought differently. He thought my life so precious that he would give himself up for me, even though I deserved the exact opposite. Having seen how undeserved this love is, I was compelled by God to turn my life around. Instead of living for myself I now live for him.

Since I committed my life to God I have had the full assurance of life in heaven and my life has a definite purpose, that of pleasing God. I don't always get it right, but I know that Jesus' death has paid the price for all I've done wrong towards God. Instead of being continually depressed, I now have complete joy, because of what Jesus did for me on the cross.

real lives

Terry is a lifeguard in Liverpool and in his spare time tells school children and youth groups about Jesus' power to change lives. His story has been reported in many countries.

Terry, why is Jesus' death so important to you?

I was an accidental pregnancy and my dad was violent towards me. I hung out with local gangs and was arrested at twelve for car theft and thirteen for drug use. I was expelled from school, sacked from my first job, and got involved with football hooliganism. After the 1985 Heysel Stadium tragedy in which thirty-nine football fans died, I was the first person charged with manslaughter, and was given a jail sentence. When I was released, I became a drug dealer. Having been raided by the police, I went on the run to Europe.

Hoping there was a better way to live, I returned to Liverpool and handed myself in. Before I was sentenced, I met some Christians who said they'd pray for me! Amazingly, my drugs case was dismissed, so I went to a local church. It wasn't what I expected – but I felt a peace and acceptance. The preacher spoke about how because of Jesus' death, God forgives us, changes us and gives us the hope of heaven. Jesus seemed to be the answer for my life. I became a Christian.

The people in church were loving and patient. My life slowly changed: eventually God broke every addiction, and physically and psychologically I recovered. God's helped me be more caring and is making me less selfish. He even restored my family relationships, and my father accepted Jesus as his saviour three days before he died. Twenty years on from Heysel, I went to Italy to apologize for what I'd done.

The death of Jesus reveals to me how much God loves me. Jesus' death in my place means a way has been made for me to become a child of God.

'Amazing love! How can it be that you, my God, should die for me?'

12. Dead or alive?

Jesus was a masterful story-teller. His biographies record many of the stories he told – stories that would have resonated with his listeners because they were so down-to-earth, but which would also have got under their skin as they tried to work out the hidden message. His stories were pithy and often humorous – and always had a point. He used them to teach about God, humans, and our relationship with God.

Looking in the mirror
In this chapter, I'd like us to listen to one of the most famous stories Jesus ever told.[1] 'There was a man who had two sons,' he began. The father in the story represents God, and the two sons denote two typical responses to God. In telling this story, Jesus is holding up a mirror for us, getting us to think about which of the two sons we are most like and whether – in relation to God – we're dead or alive.

'Dad, I wish you were dead'

> The younger one [son] said to his father, 'Father, give me my share
> of the estate.' So he divided his property between them.

For a son to go to his dad in the Middle East two thousand years
ago and ask for his share of the estate was considerably worse than
for a young man to approach his parents today and ask for a loan.
In fact, it's hard to exaggerate the shock Jesus' hearers would have
had at the opening of this story. Theirs was a society where family
ties were much stronger than in our own culture and where
property would pass from one generation to the next only as the
old one died out. The younger son in the story was so far out of
turn that it's no understatement to say that he wished his dad were
dead. He couldn't wait for his father to die before getting his hands
on the money, so he asked his dad to sell off part of the estate
instead, and pass on the inheritance early. The younger son would
have brought immense shame on the entire family.

In the previous couple of chapters, we've discovered some of the enormous implications of Jesus' resurrection. Paul always knew that God wanted to know us, but came to realize that in rejecting Jesus, he'd rejected God himself. If you like, he'd become the younger son in this story: wishing God out of the way so he could live his life how he wanted.

Are you in that position? It can be a fun position to be in, as the younger son knew:

> Not long after that, the younger son got together all he had, set off for a distant country and there squandered his wealth in wild living.

It doesn't take much imagination to work out how he spent his money. This was the original world tour, with the intention of trying everything under the sun. He only bought a one-way ticket, and he didn't bother sending any text messages home. He wasn't in the slightest bit concerned about his dad; his only concern was having a good time.

Many people are in exactly that place today. Maybe they're not rich enough to be on a round-the-world tour, but their underlying attitude is the same: living for themselves, caring nothing for God. It may well have happened unknowingly, but they've ignored God and rejected his rules, preferring to set their own boundaries for acceptable behaviour.

The shock that Jesus' listeners would have felt towards the younger son should be the shock we feel about ourselves: how outrageous to reject God! One friend of mine talks about 'practical atheists' – people who might *say* they believe in God, but their daily lives make it quite clear that they *live* as though they think him utterly irrelevant – as good as dead. In your desire to get the most out of life, have you deeply offended God by ignoring him?

Or maybe for you the party finished long ago.

'What am I playing at?'

> After he had spent everything, there was a severe famine in
> that whole country, and he began to be in need. So he went
> and hired himself out to a citizen of that country, who sent
> him to his fields to feed pigs. He longed to fill his stomach
> with the pods that the pigs were eating, but no-one gave him
> anything.

At some point in life, we all learn that the party can't go on for
ever. Ironically, the pursuit of pleasure never satisfies as we
constantly seek bigger and better experiences. When addiction
takes hold, we realize that we've been enslaved.

The younger son certainly learnt that lesson. He wasn't sure
whether his life felt more like a 4 a.m. screaming nightmare or an
8 a.m. throbbing hangover. Either way, he was deeply unhappy,
starving hungry and desperately lonely. We can tell how low he'd
fallen – the thought of eating pig food is disgusting enough for us;
for him as a Jew, having anything to do with pigs was utterly
repulsive.

It often takes some external event in our lives to make us come
to our senses. The younger son experienced physical disaster and
financial ruin. Others suddenly wake up to find themselves facing
personal failure, tragic loss, or a crippling illness. But the results are
often the same: unhappiness, emptiness and loneliness. Can you
identify with those?

The one good thing about being at rock bottom is that you can
only go in one direction – up. The question is: how?

> When he came to his senses, he said, 'How many of my father's
> hired men have food to spare, and here I am starving to death!
> I will set out and go back to my father and say to him: Father, I
> have sinned against heaven and against you. I am no longer worthy
> to be called your son; make me like one of your hired men.' So he
> got up and went to his father.

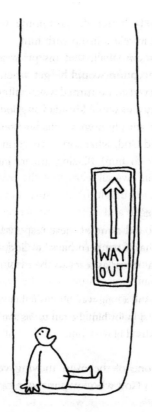

Here's the key: 'he came to his senses'. Rather than ignoring his problems, hoping against hope that they would go away of their own accord, he thought long and hard about where he had gone wrong, and what he could do to put it right. He realized that his world tour, fun though it was while it lasted, gave only temporary pleasure and no permanent security. When he'd been at home, he couldn't wait to get out, but now he knew that he'd be much better off back home.

That's the way it is between us and God: many people think that being a Christian would be a living nightmare full of petty rules and with precious little freedom. But the reality is that living away from God always results in inner turmoil. Surprising as it may sound, we'd all be better off 'back home' with God – living as he made us to live, in relationship with him.

So the younger son swallowed his pride and decided to go home. But what reception would he get when he got there? He knew that he deserved to be turned away: after all, he'd brought shame on the family and wished his dad as good as dead! The only thing he could take with him were words of humble apology.

If you've rejected God, what sort of reaction would you expect if you turned back to him? Blazing anger? Fierce judgment? A blocked entrance?

'I want you back, son'
The younger son found none of these responses, and Jesus wants us to understand that if we turn back to God, we receive such a warm welcome that it brings tears to the eyes:

> But while he was still a long way off, his father saw him and was filled with compassion for him; he ran to his son, threw his arms around him and kissed him.

To me, this is one of the most moving verses in the Bible, because it pictures a God who loves me so much that:

- he's been looking out for my return ever since I walked out on him;
- he doesn't care what other people think of me (his friends and neighbours would have been scandalized by the son's disgraceful behaviour);
- he's willing to humiliate himself (no father in those days would have stooped to the indignity of running, especially in public) – just as Jesus was humiliated on the cross;
- he doesn't mind what I look like (it's a fair guess that the younger son would have stunk to high heaven after his disgusting work and long walk home);
- he embraces me personally.

That's how much he loves you, too. Could this be the answer to our deep inner longings?

This overwhelming welcome had occurred even before the son could give his apology:

> The son said to him, 'Father, I have sinned against heaven and against you. I am no longer worthy to be called your son.'

But the father cut him off mid-sentence. True, he wasn't worthy to belong to the family after what he'd done, but it was up to the father to set the terms of welcome – and there was to be no probationary period to check that the change of heart was real:

> But the father said to his servants, 'Quick! Bring the best robe and put it on him. Put a ring on his finger and sandals on his feet. Bring the fattened calf and kill it. Let's have a feast and celebrate.

Earlier on, the son had enjoyed wild parties in distant countries, but here was the real party, one that welcomed him home not as a hired worker but as an honoured son.

And the punchline?

> 'For this son of mine was *dead* and is *alive* again; he was lost and is found.' So they began to celebrate.

Do you see? This is the incredible welcome that awaits us if we return to God, and the amazing reversal in our status when we do so. We may be spiritually dead now, but God makes us alive again.

But maybe you don't recognize yourself in the mirror so far. You're not partying; nor are you hurting. You're just working.

Out in the cold

> Meanwhile, the older son was in the field. When he came near the house, he heard music and dancing. So he called one of the servants

and asked him what was going on. 'Your brother has come,' he replied, 'and your father has killed the fattened calf because he has him back safe and sound.'

The older brother became angry and refused to go in. So his father went out and pleaded with him. But he answered his father, 'Look! All these years I've been slaving for you and never disobeyed your orders. Yet you never gave me even a young goat so I could celebrate with my friends. But when this son of yours who has squandered your property with prostitutes comes home, you kill the fattened calf for him!'

We tend to feel a bit sorry for the older son, who clearly felt hard-done by. But all the time he'd been working for his dad, he'd been missing the point. He clearly didn't love his father, so he saw his work as 'slaving'. He wasn't able to *receive* his father's love because he was trying so hard to *achieve* it.

It's an easy mistake to make. If you didn't recognize yourself in the mirror as the younger son, maybe you recognize yourself now. I suspect that if Paul had heard this story *before* his encounter with Jesus, he'd have identified with this older son: he saw God as a hard task-master so slaved away trying to earn his favour – but in doing so, missed God's heart of love.

'My son,' the father said, 'you are always with me, and everything I have is yours. But we had to celebrate and be glad, because this brother of yours was dead and is alive again; he was lost and is found.'

His dad reassured his oldest son of his love, and Jesus underlines the point again about the younger son having been dead but now found alive, before stopping the story somewhat prematurely. It was, of course, deliberate: if you identify with the older son, Jesus leaves you to finish the story. Will you *receive* God's love and join the party, or stay out in the cold, trying unsuccessfully to *earn* God's love?

Responding to God

As you look in the mirror, who do you see? Whether you see the younger son having the time of his life or sitting disconsolately by the pigsty, or whether you see the older son outside in the cold, something needs to be done. You need to come home.

real lives

Deborah is a GP whose interests include reading, entertaining and avoiding lawn mowing.

Deborah, how did you become a Christian?

I attended church from an early age. One occurrence really helped to crystallize my faith. My Sunday school teacher was recounting a memorable event from her own childhood. She'd been unwell and was sleeping in her parents' bed that night. She became anxious regarding what would happen to her if Jesus were to come again. She tried to reassure herself that should this happen she would hold on to her Mother's night-dress and be taken along with her.

Soon after having this thought she heard a voice saying to her 'It's no good, you'll have to go alone.' At that point she made her own personal commitment to being a follower of Christ.

Listening to her story, I understood clearly for the first time that God was interested in a relationship with me *first hand* ... there could be no hiding behind my mother's skirts or 'hand-me-down' Christianity. It was what I believed personally that was important. I knew at that point that I wanted to have my own special relationship with God. I began having my own personal 'talks' with God, telling him about my worries and saying sorry for the things I'd done wrong. I knew absolutely that he was always with me.

Over the years my understanding of God and how we are saved through his son Jesus has grown. At university, it would have been easy to drift away, but I always came back to what I knew was true – Jesus died for me so that I could be free from sin and know God intimately. There have been many ups and downs since but I have never forgotten the lesson that I was taught that Sunday at church. That God should desire such a personal relationship with me is a source of constant wonder.

real lives

Mark

Mark is married with five daughters, and as a social worker has been helping people with mental health concerns for the last two years. In his spare time, he coaches under sixteens' football.

Mark, how did you become a Christian?

Until five years ago, life was filled with what I thought were good times. I was at lots of parties, had lots of friends. Music was my life – I'd always wanted to DJ and make a name through playing music. I was very selfish, thinking of myself all the time with little consideration for others. I used people for lifts to the club. I cried poverty so they would buy me drinks and in return I would make them laugh. My relationships with women weren't deep or long, but I didn't want any more. For three years, I set no boundaries for myself; I was living fast but feeling little.

Then I was invited round to a friend's house for a meal. My friend told me why Jesus died on the cross, and that God had a plan for my life, if I repented and believed. I didn't understand it all, but I left feeling challenged and peculiar! I'm the sort of person who questions things, so I talked to my partner, and started going to church as I began to seek what God had in store for me. I didn't yet believe, but was encouraged by what I heard. I also attended a short course at church that told me more about Jesus. I was becoming thirsty for the truth.

About six months later I woke up in the middle of the night and while my family were asleep I went downstairs and read a chapter from one of the gospels and prayed. I said sorry to God for all the wrong I had done to him and others, and cried to the Lord for forgiveness. I knew that if I truly believed, he would forgive me because of Jesus' death on the cross. That night I became a Christian.

13. Meeting the risen Jesus

We gave one of my nephews a jigsaw puzzle for his birthday the other day. He's only three, so the puzzle was of a dinosaur, and had only five pieces. It was one of those jigsaws that come in their completed form – so to start with, my nephew did the easy task of dismantling the jigsaw, leaving his uncle to put it back together again. As he becomes more familiar with it, I'm sure the roles will reverse!

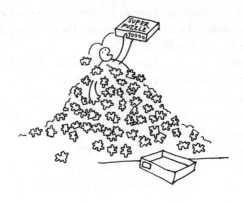

As we get older, the jigsaw puzzles become more difficult. Do you remember doing 100-piece jigsaws, then 500-piece, then 1,000-piece puzzles? In those, the pieces were all broken up, and we worked from the picture on the front of the box to complete the puzzle. I've never dared try one of those puzzles that don't even show you the picture, when you have to painstakingly work it out by matching the pieces together by shape and colour; only when you've finished do you get to see the full picture.

Seeing the big picture

In the previous few chapters we've covered a lot of ground: we've seen how Paul's life was turned around and his thinking turned upside down by realizing Jesus had been raised from the dead; and then looked in the mirror and seen where we stand before God. I've shown you lots of different pieces of the jigsaw puzzle of the Christian faith, but maybe it's not quite clear how it all fits together, or what the final picture looks like. Let me summarize where we've got to by putting the pieces in order, to help you to see and understand the big picture.

- *Jesus' life* shows us what God is like. He's full of indiscriminate compassion, reaching out to people of every age, race, background, sex and lifestyle.
- *Jesus' teaching* comes as a rude awakening. As well as great moral instruction, he gives the verdict that we are all spiritually dead because we've rejected God's rightful authority over our lives.
- *Jesus' death* was the climax of his mission. He died an innocent man, taking the punishment of the guilty. As we are the guilty people, Jesus' death offers us forgiveness of sins, freedom from guilt, healing of past hurts and the conquering of death. By faith in his death, we can be made alive and put back in touch with God.
- *Jesus' resurrection* is the best explanation for what happened to him after his dead body was put in the tomb. It is also the

only explanation for the radical change that occurred in the lives of his followers. Jesus' resurrection was God's vindication of his life and death, and tells us that Jesus is alive and watching over us now. After his resurrection, Jesus was taken up to heaven, from where he now rules the earth.

○ *Jesus will come again* to bring this world as we know it to its fulfilment. Jesus will judge all people everywhere fairly, based on our prior response to him. He will confirm our stated preference: those who've rejected him will in turn be rejected by him and experience the grim reality of hell; those who've accepted him and followed him as their Lord will enjoy the paradise of heaven – a place of eternal life not eternal boredom, from where all evil, injustice, sadness and death are banished. The height of heaven will be the privilege of living for eternity in the presence of the most amazing man who's ever lived: Jesus.

○ *God longs for us to know him* with a deep and active passion. Jesus' story in the previous chapter didn't just show us our own heart, it gave us a glimpse of God's heart as well. He loves us deeply; he longs for us to return to him; he's filled with overwhelming joy and forgiveness when we do so.

When you see those jigsaw pieces fitting together, and take a step backwards to look at the whole, what do you see? We don't find a centuries-old religious painting of the sort that you might see in an art gallery or ancient church. Those paintings are beautiful to look at (if you like that sort of thing), yet easy to walk away from. The picture that we've uncovered isn't only set in the past, but in the future as well, and includes this twenty-first century. Nor is it set only in Palestine and Israel, but encompasses every nation of the world. What's more, the picture we've uncovered isn't in two dimensions, but three. At its centre stands the risen Jesus, with his arm outstretched towards you, and his nail-scarred hand beckoning you towards him. The picture even turns out to include sound as well, with Jesus calling you by name.

It's the most incredible picture, and we instinctively know that it demands some sort of response. Think of it this way: when a man asks a woman to marry him, there are in the end only two answers – 'yes' or 'no'. The woman (we hope!) will think carefully about her response, because it's such a major decision.

Responding to God
Responding to Jesus is not so dissimilar. He asks each one of us to make a momentous decision – whether or not to align ourselves with him and follow him. As with getting married, the repercussions are huge and life-long. So what's involved in following him? Jesus used two phrases that sum it up: 'Repent and believe the good news' and 'Follow me'.[1] Let's unpack what he meant.

> **Jesus asks each one of us to make a momentous decision — whether or not to align ourselves with him and follow him.**

'Repent' – sorrow for the past
To 'repent' means to change direction. When Roman soldiers were marching along and told to 'repent', they did an about turn. If we were travelling along today, we might call it a 'U-turn'.

Literally, the word 'repent' is to do with a change of mind. So when Jesus tells us to 'repent', he's telling us to change our minds about him, and change the direction of our lives to follow him. That's exactly what the younger son did in Jesus' story. He 'came to his senses' and, realizing the mistakes he'd made, turned round to head back to his father, willing to apologize.

Repenting takes great humility. But there's no avoiding the fact that if we've rejected or ignored God thus far in our lives, the only way there can be reconciliation between us is if we're willing to say sorry to God, acknowledging both the hurt we've caused him – and how much it cost Jesus to win forgiveness for us.

'Believe the good news' – look to the cross

The next step in responding to God is to believe the good news about Jesus Christ – that he is God in human flesh, who was born into our world, lived a perfect life, suffered death in order to grant us forgiveness, rose to new life and will come again as our judge.

In common language, to say 'I believe in . . .' is a statement of what your mind thinks. In the Bible, 'belief' is much deeper than that – it involves the heart and body as well. Actions as well as words are required. An illustration will help explain this.

Suppose you have a rare form of cancer. It becomes apparent that even the country's leading specialist cannot cure you, but he says 'I know someone who can. They're based in Canada, but they have a very good success rate with curing your cancer.' What do you do? It's no good saying 'I believe that doctor can cure me' – but then staying at home in bed! That sort of belief is pointless. If you really believe the specialist, you raise the money, get on a plane and go. Similarly, a genuine Christian puts their belief about Jesus into action: they say that he's God, and then prove their belief by putting Jesus' teaching into practise day by day.

'Follow me' – change in the future

The younger son in Jesus' story understood the implications of returning to his father. In looking to be accepted back into his home as a hired worker (or, indeed, as a son), the son would be coming under his father's authority and agreeing to live by his rules. It would be no good if he carried on living the wild lifestyle of his runaway years – that would only have shown up his 'repentance' as hollow. Rather, he must put behind him all the things that would displease his father. When Paul summarized what he told people to do in response to God, he said, 'I preached that they should repent and turn to God *and prove their repentance by their deeds*.'[2]

Thus, 'Following Jesus' turns out to have huge implications for our lives. Jesus' own way of saying this was brutally clear but distinctly unappealing! 'If anyone would come after me,' he said, 'they must deny themselves and take up their cross and follow me.'[3]

'Denying self' means saying 'no' to our own desires, ambitions and priorities, and asking instead, 'What would Jesus want?' It's to put Jesus' interests above our own. When I got married, I had to give up my autonomy – my freedom to make decisions based on what *I* wanted. Instead, I had to start thinking about my *wife* as well, and not just by putting her desires and needs *alongside* my own, but trying to put them *above* my own. To follow Jesus is to make him number one in our life, rather than ourselves – and that applies to every area of life.

In time, Jesus will scrutinize our heart, looking at the way we conduct our relationships. At some point, he'll have a look at our mind – the way we think. He'll want to examine our mouths (what

we say), our eyes (what we look at and read), our ears (what we listen to). He'll want to enter our pockets, to help us change how we use our money. He'll look at our hands and feet, to see how we use our bodies physically. Slowly, he'll look at every part of our lives, and prompt us about changes we need to make if we're serious about following him.

'Denying self' is hard work, but Jesus is realistic about the task:

- He doesn't expect every change to happen *instantly* and certainly doesn't wait for us to be perfect before accepting us. Change is a life-long process.
- He doesn't expect change to happen *alone*, but helps us. New Year's resolutions tend to fail because we attempt to keep them by using our own strength. Christians have God's help to change – the same helping power that raised Christ from the dead![4]

Because we have God's help, the changes required by following Jesus aren't impossible. The 'Real Lives' stories in this book show that God really does turn ordinary people's lives around, helping us to break powerful addictions, overcome crippling fears and find a healthy self-image.

At first hearing, accepting Jesus' invitation to 'deny ourselves' would seem to be idiotic. However, he then gave us an eternal perspective on his invitation: 'For whoever wants to save their life will lose it, but whoever loses their life for me and for the gospel will save it. What good is it for a person to gain the whole world, yet forfeit their soul? Or what can a person give in exchange for their soul?'[5] He's making the point that hanging on to our own life now (by denying him) will ultimately lead to rejection by him eternally. We might gain the world and all its riches for our three score years and ten, but we'll lose our soul eternally – a fate that far outweighs any temporary benefits this world might give. By contrast, 'losing' our own life now (by putting Jesus first) leads to being accepted into his family – permanently. When viewed from an eternal perspective, Jesus' invitation isn't as crazy as it first seemed. In fact, it becomes clear that the sensible thing to do is to accept his invitation. The really crazy person is the one who turns him down.

Indeed, followers of Jesus find that his promise of 'life in all its fullness'[6] is accurate when compared to their former life: we experience an intimate friendship with our creator that we were made to have; deeper relationships as we join a new family; greater purpose in life in serving Jesus; a clearer and more enriching identity in being God's child; a hope for the future that is infinitely firmer than wishful thinking – the list could go on. There are real costs in following Jesus but the benefits are out of this world.[7]

Paul's experience was that becoming a Christian was the best decision he ever made: 'Christ has shown me that what I once thought was valuable is worthless. Nothing is as wonderful as knowing Christ Jesus my Lord. I have given up everything else and count it all as garbage. All I want is Christ and to know that I belong to him.'[8] I decided to follow Jesus years ago, and have never regretted it for a moment either. But what will your decision be?

Making a decision

It's right to make a carefully considered response, for it's a decision that will shape the rest of your life. But as you consider whether to become a Christian, remember also the implications of *not* doing so. One man eloquently described his moment of decision like this:

There is a gap between the probable and the proved. How was I to cross it? If I were to stake my whole life on the risen Christ, I wanted proof. I wanted certainty. I wanted to see him eat a bit of fish. I wanted letters of fire across the sky. I got none of these. And I continued to hang about on the edge of the gap ... It was a question of whether to accept him – or reject. My God! There was a gap behind me as well! Perhaps the leap to acceptance was a horrifying gamble – but what of the leap to rejection? There might be no certainty that Christ was God – but, by God, there was no

certainty that he was not. This was not to be borne. I could not
reject Jesus. There was only one thing to do once I had seen the gap
behind me. I turned away from it, and flung myself over the gap
towards Jesus.'[9]

Some people reading this book might genuinely need more
time to think about the costs involved – but please don't delay the
decision for too long. You might find it useful to attend an Alpha
course or a Christianity Explored course or some other Christian
basics course in a local church to help you come to your decision.[10]
Jesus offers us a wonderful gift and life-long friendship, but just
as the man who's proposed to a woman may allow her some time
to think carefully, he eventually requires a straight 'yes' or 'no'
answer.

Some people think that they can put off their moment of
believing until just before they die. Yet although God will readily
accept 'death-bed conversions', not all of us know when we'll die,
and whether we'll have time to 'repent and believe' at that point.
In any case, how can anyone delay receiving the most precious gift
we can ever receive, having genuinely understood how much it
cost Jesus to buy? It would be the height of insolence! Those who
want to delay committing themselves to Jesus have not fully
understood the perilous predicament they are in. The very name
'Jesus' means 'The Lord saves' or 'The Lord rescues'[11] – and a
drowning man wants to be rescued as soon as possible, not for it to
be put off as long as possible.

The very name 'Jesus' means 'The Lord saves' or 'The Lord rescues'.

Far from delaying our decision, the Bible urges us to get right
with God as soon as possible. 'Seek the Lord while he may be found;
call on him while he is near.' 'Today, if you hear his voice, do not

harden your hearts.' 'Now is the time of God's favour, now is the day of salvation.'[12] If you're ready to become a Christian, do so!

Meeting the risen Jesus

The way to tell Jesus that you want to become a Christian is by speaking to him. It doesn't matter whether you speak out loud, or quietly in your mind – he's God, so he'll be able to hear you. Speaking to God (often called prayer) may feel strange at first, but will become quite natural with time. In your prayer, you'll want to make it clear that you're repenting (doing the U-turn: turning *away* from selfish rejection of God, and turning *to* Christ), that you believe in him, and that you're committed to putting that belief into action from now on by following him. If there are things in your past that make you feel particularly guilty, it will be worth mentioning them specifically, and asking for God's forgiveness, confident that he will give it. You might want to base your prayer on this one, adding in your own personal confessions in the blanks:

> Jesus,
> I now recognize that you are God,
> yet that I have rebelled against you.
> I'm sorry for the wrong ways I've treated you [. . .]
> I'm sorry for the wrong ways I've treated other people [. . .]
> Please forgive me.
> Thank you so much for loving me and dying for me on the cross.
> I believe that through your death,
> my relationship with you can start over again.
> Please help me to stop going my own way
> and start following you. Amen.

('Amen' means 'I agree'. Saying it is like signing your name at the bottom of a letter or petition – it's saying that you agree with these words.)

If you've made that prayer your own, the chances are you don't feel any different, but that's not to say your prayer hasn't 'worked'.

Indeed, it's always dangerous to trust our feelings as some sort of spiritual barometer. Our feelings about how we're doing as a Christian go up and down, just as our feelings about the rest of life are very changeable. Our faith rests on God's promises, not our feelings – and God's promises are firm and solid. So let me finish with a reminder of some of God's promises:

- 'Whoever comes to me I will never drive away.'[13] This reassures us that Jesus welcomes everyone who comes to him.
- 'For God so loved the world that he gave his one and only Son, that whoever believes in him shall not perish but have eternal life.'[14] This reminds us of God's deep love for us.
- 'If we confess our sins to God, he can always be trusted to forgive us and take our sins away.'[15] This assures us that God has pardoned us and completely forgotten about our previous rejection of him.
- 'I am the resurrection and the life. Those who believe in me will live, even though they die; and whoever lives and believes in me will never die.'[16] Based on Jesus' own victory over death, this reassures us of life beyond the grave.

Is *Jesus* dead or alive? The evidence of his empty tomb and the changed lives of his followers both then and now declare that he's alive.

Are *you* dead or alive? Jesus said, 'I tell you the truth, whoever hears my word and believes him who sent me has eternal life and will not be condemned; they have crossed over from death to life.'[17]

Congratulations!

Postscript: What next?

If you've become a Christian, welcome to the family! I've made it clear that it's a decision that will affect the rest of your life – for the better. But what should you do over the next few days?

After the first ever Christian sermon, 'Those who accepted [the] message were baptised ... They devoted themselves to the apostles' teaching and to the fellowship, to the breaking of bread and to prayer.'[1] These first converts set a good pattern for someone's first steps as a Christian. Let me briefly highlight what those steps were and give you some Bible passages to look at. I strongly recommend reading one or more of the books from the 'Further reading' list as well.

1. Go public
As a new Christian, you must make some sort of public declaration of your new faith – it's a way of nailing your colours to the mast. To start with, tell a friend (maybe a Christian you know?) what you've done. Often, telling someone else makes your decision seem more real to you as well. In due course, when you've settled

in a local church, you may need to be baptized (an initiation ceremony with water symbolizing cleansing from sin) as a further public declaration of your new faith.

'Going public' with your faith is an ongoing part of the Christian life. Having received such a precious gift ourselves, and knowing that it's freely available to all, it would be greedy not to tell others! It can be daunting to speak about our faith, especially at first, and we will encounter much opposition and even rejection as we do so, but God helps us. People will see your life changing and ask questions – they can be good opportunities to give credit to God. A word of warning: it can be easy to come across as judgmental when telling people they need to become Christians, especially if that person already thinks of themselves as a Christian. 'Gentleness' and 'respect' are to be our hallmarks when speaking to others about Jesus.

Some Bible passages to read on going public: Matthew 28.18–20; 1 Peter 3.15–16.

2. Listen to God

The new Christians then 'devoted themselves to the apostles' teaching' – teaching that we now find in the Bible. Christians believe that the Bible is God's word to us, and that by reading and studying the Bible, we hear God speaking to us. We must listen to him for guidance about how our life needs to be reformed, and what direction our life should take. The first Christian converts 'devoted' themselves to such teaching, and so should we. Make time each day to read the Bible, asking that God will help you to understand it and live it.

Strange as it sounds, don't start reading the Bible at the beginning! The Bible is a library not a single book, and in a library, we wouldn't read from one end of the bookshelf to the other. Start by reading one or two of the gospels, then the rest of the New Testament. Get a modern translation of the Bible that you find easy to understand. Investing in some Bible reading notes will help you get into the habit of daily Bible reading, and help you to understand and apply what you're reading.[2]

Some Bible passages to read on the Bible: 2 Timothy 3.14–16; Psalm 119.97–106.

3. Join in the family activities

As a new Christian, you should join a local church, because belonging to a church is a key part of keeping going and growing as a Christian. A good church will teach the Bible carefully, applying it to everyday life, encouraging people to grow in the Christian faith. It will be a place for getting to know people well in smaller groups through the week as well as on Sundays. A good church will also focus strongly on Jesus' death on the cross in its practise and preaching – that is what the strange-sounding practise of 'the breaking of bread' refers to.

A good way to get to know people in your new church, and to go over the basics of the Christian faith again, is to join a group for new Christians or those considering the Christian faith. These are informal groups where lots of questions can be asked. When you visit a church, introduce yourself to the minister, explain that you've recently become a Christian, and ask if they have a group like that (see www.alpha.org or www.christianityexplored.com if you're struggling to find a group).

Some Bible passages to read on belonging to a church: Romans 12.3–13; Acts 2.42–47.

4. Talk to God

Prayer is talking to God from your heart. God doesn't mind whether you use proper English or not – like any father, he just longs to hear from his children, and to answer their prayers. However, just as a loving parent doesn't always give their child what they ask for, nor will God, because not everything we ask for is actually good for us. In time, it will become more obvious what sort of things you should ask for in prayer. 'ACTS' is a useful mnemonic in structuring prayer:

Adoration – praising God for who he is and what he's done.

Confession – saying sorry to God for the wrong things you've done recently, and asking for his forgiveness and his help in not repeating them.

Thanksgiving – thanking God for his good gifts to you, such as health, family, church, etc.

Supplication – asking God to intervene in particular situations. You should pray for yourselves, your friends, and wider world concerns.

An obvious time to pray by yourself is before and after you've read the Bible each day – but you can carry on praying short prayers through the day while on the bus or doing the washing up! It can be very encouraging to pray with others as well – this might happen in church gatherings.

Some Bible passages to read on prayer: Luke 11.1–13; 18.1–14.

Further reading

Chapter 1: Is there anybody out there?
John Dickson, *If I Were God, I'd Make Myself Clearer*
(Matthias Media, 2003).
Michael Green and Nick Spencer, *I'd Like to Believe, But . . .*
(IVP, 2005) – especially chapter 12.
Alister McGrath, *Glimpsing the Face of God* (Lion, 2002).
Ravi Zacharias, *Can Man Live Without God?* (Authentic,
1995).

Chapter 2: Why hasn't God done something about all the suffering?
John Dickson, *If I Were God, I'd End All the Pain* (Matthias
Media, 2003).
Alister McGrath, *Why Does God Allow Suffering?* (Hodder, 2000).
Philip Yancey, *Where is God When it Hurts?* (Zondervan, 2003).

Chapter 3: What happens when we die?
Adrian Holloway, *The Shock of Your Life* (Kingsway, 2000).
David Lawrence, *Heaven . . . It's Not the End of the World!*
(Scripture Union, 1995).
Alec Motyer, *After Death* (Christian Focus, 1996).
David Watson, *Fear No Evil* (Hodder, 1985).

Chapter 4: Does life have a meaning or purpose?
Nicky Gumbel, *Questions of Life* (Kingsway, 2003).
Vaughan Roberts, *Turning Points* (Authentic, 1999).

Chapter 5: Which religion, if any, is true?

Martin Goldsmith, *What About Other Faiths?* (Hodder, 1999).
Michael Green, *But Don't All Religions Lead to God?* (IVP, 2002).
Ravi Zacharias, *Jesus Among Other Gods* (STL, 2000).

Chapter 6: Looking at the evidence

On sources of evidence from outside the Bible about early Christianity:
Paul Barnett, *Is the New Testament History?* (Paternoster, 1986).
F.F. Bruce, *The New Testament Documents: Are They Reliable?*,
   6th ed. (IVP, 1981).
Gary Habermas, *The Historical Jesus: Ancient Evidence for the Life
   of Christ* (College Press, 1996).
On how the four gospel accounts for the Easter weekend fit together:
Peter Walker, *The Weekend That Changed the World* (Marshall
   Pickering, 1999).
John Wenham, *Easter Enigma* (Paternoster Press, 1992).

Chapter 7: Is the evidence reliable?

Paul Barnett, *Is the New Testament History?* (Paternoster, 1986).
Craig Blomberg, *The Historical Reliability of the Gospels* (IVP, 1987).
F.F. Bruce, *The New Testament Documents: Are They Reliable?*,
   6th ed. (IVP, 1981).
Michael Green, *The Books the Church Suppressed* (Monarch, 2005).
Amy Orr-Ewing, *Why Trust the Bible?* (IVP, 2005).
Lee Strobel, *The Case for Christ* (Zondervan, 1998).

Chapter 8: Dead . . . ?

On some of the popular alternative theories that have been suggested:
Michael Green, *The Books the Church Suppressed* (Monarch, 2005).
Tom Wright, *Who was Jesus?* (SPCK, 1992).
Close investigations into the evidence for the resurrection:
Josh McDowell, *The Resurrection Factor* (Paternoster, 1993).
Frank Morison, *Who Moved the Stone?* (Faber & Faber, 1930, with
   frequent reprints since).
Lee Strobel, *The Case for Christ* (Zondervan, 1998).

Published debates between high-profile 'supporters' and 'opponents' of Jesus' resurrection:

Gary Habermas and Anthony Flew, *Did Jesus Rise From the Dead?: The Resurrection Debate* (HarperCollins, 1987).

Ronald Copan and Paul Tacelli (editors), *Jesus' Resurrection: Fact or Figment? A debate between William Lane Craig and Gerd Ludemann* (IVP USA, 2000).

Chapter 9: or alive?

As for chapter 8. In addition, on how science and Christian faith relate to each other:

Alister McGrath, *Dawkins' God* (Blackwell, 2004).

John Polkinghorne, *Belief in God in an Age of Science* (Yale Nota Bene, 2003).

For non-scientists:

Nicky Gumbel, *Is There a Conflict Between Science and Christianity?* (Kingsway, 2002).

Chapter 10: What are the implications of Jesus' resurrection?

Michael Green, *Who is this Jesus?* (Kingsway, 2004).

J. John and Chris Walley, *The Life: A Portrait of Jesus* (Authentic, 2004).

Chapter 11: Life from death

Alister McGrath, *Making Sense of the Cross* (IVP, 1992).

Mark Meynell, *Cross-examined* (IVP, 2001).

Rico Tice and Barry Cooper, *Christianity Explored* (Authentic, 2002).

Chapter 12: Dead or alive?

Philip Yancey, *What's So Amazing About Grace?* (Zondervan, 2002).

Chapter 13: Meeting the risen Jesus

John Chapman, *A Fresh Start* (Matthias Media, 1997).

Vaughan Roberts, *Turning Points* (Authentic, 1999).

Postscript: What next?

Phillip Jensen, *Just for Starters* (Matthias Media, 2003).

Vaughan Roberts, *Distinctives* (Authentic, 2000).

See also various *Pathway Bible Guides* published by The Goodbook Company (www.thegoodbook.co.uk).

Glossary

Agnostic – someone who isn't sure whether or not there is a god, or who believes it is impossible to know if there is a god

Anoint – to apply oils or other ointments to a person. Jesus' body was anointed after his death as part of Jewish burial customs

Assurance – Christian assurance refers to the confidence a believer has of being accepted by God, despite our sin. Such assurance is based not on a believer's efforts, but on God's promise

Atheist – someone who believes there is no god

Baptism/baptizing – a Christian initiation rite involving the application of water to the head or immersion of the body into water, which symbolizes the cleansing from sin that faith in Jesus results in

Belief system – the set of beliefs by which someone lives their life. Also called 'worldview'

Bible – the Christian sacred writings, comprising the Old and New Testaments

Blasphemy – to speak of God in an unworthy way. As a specific charge made against Jesus, it refers to his supposedly false claim to be God

Christ – a title rather than a surname. See *Messiah*

Christian – someone who follows Jesus as the Christ (i.e. their King

Creation – the world as originally made by God. Which 'method' (e.g. evolution) he used is irrelevant to this current work

Crucifixion – a Roman method of execution, widely regarded as one of the most painful ever invented (see chapter 6)

Easter – the remembrance and celebration of the period around
   Jesus' death and resurrection
Easter Day – the day on which Jesus rose from the dead
Evil – morally bad or wrong, as judged by God
god – a divine being. 'God' (capital G) is the Christian
   understanding of God, based on his self-revelation in
   history as loving, just, holy, personal, patient, faithful, etc.
Good Friday – the name given to the day on which Jesus
   died
Gospel – (1) 'a gospel' is a literary term, referring to one of
   the biographies of Jesus; (2) 'the gospel' (literally, 'the
   good news') is the message about Jesus as preached by him
   and his followers
Heaven – the sphere of existence, unseen to the human eye,
   where God lives. Strictly speaking, the Bible doesn't say that
   anyone 'goes to heaven' when they die. Rather, those who
   believe and trust in Jesus will join him in his new creation
   after they've faced God's judgment
Hell – as taught by Jesus, the place where all who don't believe
   and trust in him go when they die, having faced God's
   judgment
Humanist – someone with a belief system that affirms the
   dignity of all humans and denies the reality of anything
   supernatural
Incarnate – embodied in human form. When Christians talk
   about Jesus being 'God incarnate' they mean that he is God
   come to earth as a human
Jesus – a man born in Bethlehem about 4 BC, who died around
   AD 30, who claimed to be the Son of God, and gave
   convincing proof that he'd been raised from the dead three
   days after being put to rest in a tomb. Sometimes known as
   Jesus of Nazareth
Kingdom of heaven – the reign of God over all things, as taught by
   Jesus. Also called 'kingdom of God'
Martyr – someone who is killed for not renouncing their beliefs

Messiah – popularly, a saviour or liberator. In the Bible, the
    Messiah is God's promised, chosen one, a king. The word
    Messiah (Hebrew) is the same as Christ (Greek)

Miracle – any event which evokes great admiration, or which
    cannot otherwise be explained by the laws of nature.
    In the Bible, miracles are understood to be unusual works
    of God

New creation – Jesus' re-creation of our present world, to
    happen at some point in the future when Jesus returns.
    The new creation will be a perfect place, unlike our current
    world

New Testament – the second part of the Christian Bible,
    explaining Jesus as the fulfilment of the Old Testament.
    See also *Old Testament*

Numinous – supernatural, mysterious

Old Testament – the Jewish sacred writings, which comprise the
    first part of the Christian Bible, written before Jesus was born.
    See also *New Testament*

Other (The) – a philosophical notion of something or someone
    radically different and superior to oneself

Prayer – talking with God

Purgatory – (as taught by the Roman Catholic church) an
    intermediate destination after death, supposedly where souls
    on their way to heaven are purged of their sin. The author
    does not share this view

Reincarnation – the rebirth of the soul in another body, a concept
    believed by Hindus, Buddhists, Sikhs and others

Resurrection – rising again from death to permanent life

Sabbath – Jewish day of rest, from sunset on Friday to sunset on
    Saturday

Sacred – set apart for, or by, God

Son of Man – Jesus' own title for himself, indicating that he saw
    himself as the fulfilment of a prophecy from the Old
    Testament about the coming of a supreme king with eternal
    dominion and universal domain

Spirituality – a way of thinking, or practice, that relates to the 'spiritual' side of life – connecting us with either an 'inner spirit' or some larger external 'spirit'

Supernatural – something outside the natural, physical realm we can see

Worship – literally, to give worth to; to honour, adore and love as a god

Notes

Introduction
1 After 'One solitary life', originally written by James Allan Francis in 1926, but used and adapted widely since.
2 1 Corinthians 15.14–15, 17–19 (CEV).
3 Acts 17.18; 2.39.

Chapter 1: Is there anybody out there?
1 Interview with Andrew Neil in *The Sunday Times* (quoted in Vaughan Roberts, *Turning Points* (Authentic, 1999), pp. 48–49).
2 Mark 1.22.
3 Mark 2.12.
4 Mark 5.42.
5 Mark 4.41.
6 Mark 3.22.
7 Mark 2.7.
8 Matthew 28.9.
9 John 20.24–28.
10 Romans 1.4; Colossians 1.15–19; Philippians 2.6.
11 E.g. Matthew 9.36; 14.14; 15.32; 20.34; Mark 1.41; Luke 19.41; John 11.33–38.
12 You'd need to read all of the gospels to see this variety – which would be no bad thing!
13 E.g. Luke 8.43–48; 19.1–9.
14 E.g. Mark 15.40–41; Luke 8.2–3; 10.38–42; John 4.6–9, 27; 11.5.
15 John 1.18.

Chapter 2: Why hasn't God done something about all the suffering?
1 Psalm 44.23–24.
2 Isaiah 53.3.

3 Paragraph adapted from John Stott, *The Cross of Christ* (IVP, 1986), p. 329.

4 From Edward Shillito, 'Jesus of the Scars', quoted by William Temple in his *Reading in St John's Gospel*, p. 385.

5 Stott, *The Cross of Christ*, pp. 335–336.

6 Hebrews 2.17–18 (The Message).

7 2 Corinthians 1.3–4.

8 Hebrews 2.14.

9 Acts 2.24.

10 Hebrews 2.9.

11 1 Corinthians 15.54–55, 57 (my italics).

12 Revelation 21.1, 3–5.

Chapter 3: What happens when we die?

1 Quoted by Chris Sinkinson in *The World's Religions – A Matter of Life and Death*, 2002, taken from www.damaris.org, 27/10/06 © Damaris Trust, 1997–2004.

2 1 Corinthians 15.20, 22–23.

3 Matthew 13.49–50.

4 C.S. Lewis, *The Great Divorce* (Fount, 1997 edition), p. 3.

5 Matthew 13.44–46.

6 1 Corinthians 2.9.

7 Revelation 7.9.

8 Revelation 21.4.

9 Revelation 21.3–4.

10 1 Corinthians 13.12.

11 Mark 8.34–38.

12 1 Thessalonians 4.13–14.

13 John 11.25–26.

14 Hebrews 2.14–15.

15 David Watson, *Fear No Evil* (Hodder & Stoughton, 1984), pp. 43, 45, 168, 172.

Chapter 4: Does life have a meaning or purpose?

1 Interviewed in the *Sunday Times* News Review, 21 October 2004.

2 Bernard Levin, 'Life's Great Riddle, and No Time to Find its Meaning', quoted by Nicky Gumbel, *Questions of Life* (Kingsway, 2001), p. 13.

3 Douglas Coupland, *Girlfriend in a Coma* (Flamingo, 1998), pp. 70–71, 76, 81.

4 Prince Charles, quoted by Rico Tice.

5 Bernard Levin, quoted in Nicky Gumbel, *Questions of Life*, pp. 13–14.

6 Interviewed in *The Times*, 15 September 1998.

7 An ancient saying, quoted several times in the Bible (e.g. Isaiah 22.13).

8 John 10.10.

9 Luke 12.15–21.

10 Barry Humphreys *More please*, quoted in Rico Tice, *Christianity Explained* (All Souls, 1999), p. 61.

11 Quoted in Alister McGrath, *Bridge Building* (IVP, 1992), p. 20.

12 Luke 12.33.

13 Matthew 6.33.

14 Philippians 4.12.

15 Interview shortly before his death, quoted in Nicky Gumbel *Questions of Life*, p. 15.

16 2 Chronicles 20.7.

17 John 17.3.

18 Matthew 6.9.

19 Philippians 3.8.

20 Exodus 34.6–7.

21 Luke 15.20, 23.

22 Selwyn Hughes, *Light on Life's Ultimate Questions* (CWR, 2002), p. 27.

23 Augustine, *Confessions*, I.1 (1).

24 John 6.35.

Chapter 5: Which religion, if any, is true?

1 I first heard this comparison of the leaders of world religions from former Baptist minister Roy Clements.

2 Galatians 6.14.

3 Chapter 7 will assess the reliability of these accounts in much more detail.

4 Romans 1.4.

5 C.S. Lewis, *God in the Dock* (Fontana, 1979) p. 81.

6 Matthew 26.63–64.

7 Michael Green, *The Empty Cross of Jesus* (Hodder, 1984), pp. 129–130.

Chapter 6: Looking at the evidence

1 Flavius Josephus, *Antiquities of the Jews*, xviii.63, translated by William Whiston (Wordsworth Editions, 2006). In one translated edition of Josephus' *Jewish War*, the writer makes reference to 'a king who did not reign', who did miracles and broke the Sabbath laws, resisted popular pressure to lead an uprising against the Romans, and was crucified by the Jews. While most scholars dismiss this particular account as unoriginal, that is by no means certain.

2 Josephus, *Antiquities*, xviii.63.

3 Cornelius Tacitus, *Annals of Imperial Rome*, xv.44, translated by M. Grant (Penguin, 1989).

4 Josephus, *Antiquities*, xviii.63.

5 Tacitus, *Annals*, xv.44.

6 Phlegon, a second-century Greek historian, whose writing is known by its quotation in Origen's *Against Celsus*, suggests that Jesus prophesied; that the darkness and earthquakes around the time of Jesus' death and resurrection did happen in Tiberius' reign; and that Jesus was crucified and rose again. The Jewish *Talmud* says that Jesus was executed on Passover Eve. Pliny, in the early second century, described Christians as 'worshipping Christ as God'.

7 Throughout this section, I will draw heavily from the gospel accounts: Matthew 26 – 28; Mark 14 – 16; Luke 22 – 24; John 18 – 21. To see how the four separate accounts of the entire weekend can be pieced together, see the books in the 'Further reading' section. There are various films that attempt to portray Jesus' death accurately, notably Mel Gibson's *The Passion of the Christ* (2004) and Franco Zeffirelli's *Jesus of Nazareth* (1977).

8 From Peter Walker, *The Weekend that Changed the World* (Marshall Pickering, 1999), p. 36, based on Martin Hengel, *Crucifixion* (SCM, 1977) and P. Connolly, *Living in the Time of Jesus of Nazareth* (Oxford University Press, revised edition 1994).

9 In addition to the gospel passages mentioned above, this section and the next also draw on 1 Corinthians 15.5–8.

10 E.g. Matthew 9.18, 23–26; Luke 7.12–15; John 11.17, 41–44.

11 Acts 9.1–9; 1 Corinthians 15.8.

Chapter 7: Is the evidence reliable?

1 Some scholars suggest much earlier dates even than this. For example, Paul Barnett, *The Truth about Jesus* (Aquila Press, 1994), estimates that they were written within *forty* years of Jesus' resurrection. John Robinson, who had previously thought the gospels were written up to one hundred years after the events, re-examined the evidence and concluded that they were finished within *thirty* years. See John Robinson, *Redating the New Testament* (SCM, 1976). John Wenham, *Redating Matthew, Mark and Luke* (Hodder & Stoughton, 1991), reckons they were written within *twenty* years!

2 1 Corinthians 15.6.

3 Craig Blomberg in Lee Strobel, *The Case for Christ* (Zondervan, 1998), pp. 42–44.

4 Luke 1.1–2 provides evidence for this.

5 Luke 1.1–4.

6 F.F. Bruce, *The New Testament Documents: Are They Reliable?* (IVP, 1981), p. 82.

7 Bruce, pp. 90–91.

8 E.M. Blaiklock, *The Acts of the Apostles* (Tyndale, 1959), p. 89.

9 Josephus, *Antiquities*, xviii.117ff.

10 Acts 24 – 25.

11 Tacitus, *Annals*, xv.44.

12 John 5.2.

13 See the suggested 'Further reading' for this chapter to examine in more detail the textual and archaeological supporting evidence to the gospels.

14 Ken Handley, 'A lawyer looks at the resurrection' in *Kategoria* (1999), vol. 15, p. 14.

15 Sir Edward Clarke to E.L. Macassey, quoted in John Stott, *Basic Christianity* (IVP, 1971), p. 47.

16 Simon Greenleaf, *The Testimony of the Evangelists Examined by the Rules of Evidence Administered in Courts of Justice*, p. vii, quoted in Strobel, *The Case for Christ*, p. 46. Professor Greenleaf's work is freely available on the web, and was reprinted by Krugel in 1995.

17 E.g. Matthew 26.69–75.

18 Matthew 28.5–9; Mark 16.1–8; Luke 24.1–11; John 20.1, 10–18.

19 The quotes in this section are from pages 317 and 331–340 of Dan Brown's *The Da Vinci Code* (Corgi, 2004). Despite claiming at the beginning to be accurate in all its details, numerous books and articles have been written refuting and correcting its claims. Even some of the tourist sites mentioned in the book now dispute its claims, despite greatly increased visitor numbers! The 'Further reading' section lists some of the accessible books written by scholars rebuffing Dan Brown's accuracy. I draw particularly on Michael Green's *The Books the Church Suppressed*.

20 Again, please see the 'Further reading' section for answers to more detailed questions.

21 John Robinson, *Can We Trust the New Testament?* (Mowbray, 1977), quoted in John Young, *The Case Against Christ* (Hodder & Stoughton, 1994), pp. 86–87.

22 F.F. Bruce, *The New Testament Documents*, p. 10.

Chapter 8: Dead . . . ?

1   Paul Schellenberger and Richard Andrews, *The Tomb of God: The Body of Jesus and the Solution to a 2000-year-old mystery* (Little Brown, 1996).

2   Dan Brown, *The Da Vinci Code* (Corgi, 2004).

3   Barbara Thiering, *Jesus the Man: A New Interpretation from the Dead Sea Scrolls* (Doubleday, 1992).

4   N.T. Wright, *Who Was Jesus?* (SPCK, 1992), p. 33. This book gives a detailed critique of Barbara Thiering's work in chapter 2.

5   Matthew 27.30–32.

6   John 19.31–33.

7   John 19.34.

8   See Lee Strobel, *The Case for Christ* (Zondervan, 1998), pp. 198–199 for a medical explanation of this.

9   Mark 15.44–45.

10 Matthew 27.60.

11 D.F. Strauss, *The Life of Jesus for the People* (Williams & Norgate, 1879), vol. 1, p. 412.

12 Mark 15.47 – 16.2.

13 Matthew 27.57–60.

14 Matthew 27.62–66.

15 Geza Vermes, *Jesus the Jew: A Historian's Reading of the Gospels* (Collins, 1973), quoted in Kel Richards, *Jesus on Trial* (Matthias Media, 2001), p. 39.

16 Charles Colson, *Loving God* (Marshalls, 1984), p. 69, quoted in Ross Clifford, *Leading Lawyers' Case for the Resurrection* (CILTPP, 1991), p. 126.

17 G.R. Beasley-Murray, *Christ is Alive* (Lutterworth Press, 1947), p. 63.

18 John 20.5–7.

19 A.N. Wilson, *Jesus* (Sinclair-Stevenson, 1992).

20 See for example, Acts 15.

21 1 Corinthians 15.7.

22 Wright, *Who Was Jesus?*, p. 61. Chapter 3 of this book goes into some depth explaining why Wilson's theories on Jesus' resurrection are not credible.

23 Matthew 28.11–15.

24 Matthew 26.56.

25 Acts 4.

26 Acts 7.54 – 8.4.

27 For example, Luke 24.30; John 20.27; John 21.13.

28 1 Corinthians 15.6.

29 See Strobel, *The Case for Christ*, pp. 238–240.

30 John 20.24–28.

31 Luke 24.36–43.

32 Frank Morison, *Who Moved the Stone?* (Faber and Faber, 1930), p. 192. The most recent edition is published by Authentic Lifestyle, 1996.

33 Morison, *Who Moved the Stone?*, pp. 9, 11.

34 Morison, *Who Moved the Stone?*, p. 89.

35 Morison, *Who Moved the Stone?*, quotes taken from Preface and Chapter 1.

Chapter 9: or alive?

1 Sir Arthur Conan Doyle, *The Sign of Four* (Spencer Blacket, 1890).

2 R.J. Berry in a letter to *The Times*, 13 July 1984.

3 Famous scientists with a Christian faith have included Nicolaus Copernicus, Galileo Galilei, Sir Isaac Newton, Michael Faraday, Robert Boyle, Joseph Lister and Louis Pasteur. The relationship between science and Christian faith is a massive topic which can't

be discussed in detail here. The 'Further reading' list includes some suggestions for those who want to take this further.

4 Michael Green, *The Empty Cross of Jesus* (Hodder and Stoughton, 1984), p. 105.

5 Acts 17.32.

6 Acts 26.8.

7 Richard Swinburne, *The Resurrection of God Incarnate* (OUP, 2003), p. 187.

8 Swinburne, p. 214.

9 John Warwick Montgomery, *Where is History Going?* (Bethany Fellowship, 1967), p. 71, quoted in Josh McDowell, *The Resurrection Factor* (Paternoster, 1993), p. 32.

10 Paul Maier in Long Beach, California's *Independent Press-Telegram*, 21 April 1973, p. A-10, quoted in McDowell, *The Resurrection Factor*, p. 22.

11 Thomas Arnold, *Sermons on the Christian Life* (Fellowes, 1842), p. 342, quoted in McDowell, p. 21.

12 The story of the beginnings of the Church is told in Acts 2 – 8. That 'the word spread' and 'the church grew in numbers' is a constant refrain, e.g. Acts 2.41; 4.4; 9.31; 16.5; 19.20.

13 The early preaching of the gospel in Acts is notable for its emphasis on eyewitness reports of Jesus' resurrection, e.g. Acts 2.32; 3.15; 4.10; 5.30–32; 10.40–41; 13.30–31.

14 N.T. Wright, *The Resurrection of the Son of God* (SPCK, 2003).

15 From N.T. Wright 'Jesus' resurrection and Christian origins', the McCarthy Lecture delivered on 13 March 2002, in the Faculty of Theology of the Gregorian University. Author's italics.

16 N.T. Wright, *New Heavens and New Earth* (Grove, 1999), p. 4.

17 Sir Edward Clarke to E.L. Macassey, quoted in J.R.W. Stott, *Basic Christianity* (IVP, 1971), p. 47.

18 Lord Darling, quoted in Michael Green, *The Day Death Died* (IVP, 1982), p. 15.

19 Val Grieve, *Your Verdict* (STL/IVP 1988), p. 17.

20 Quoted in Wilbur Smith, *Therefore Stand* (Baker, 1972), p. 425.

21 Chief Baron Pollock to the jury in *Regina v Exall*, quoted in Ken Handley, 'A Lawyer Looks at the Resurrection', in *Kategoria* no. 15 (1999), Matthias Media, p. 20.

22 Acts 5.34–39.

23 John 20.29.

24 *The Guinness Book of Records 1990*, p. 211.

25 Lionel Luckhoo, *What is Your Verdict?* (Fellowship Press, 1984), p. 19, quoted in Ross Clifford, *Leading Lawyers' Case for the Resurrection* (CILTPP, 1996), p. 112.

26 Quotes from Lionel Luckhoo, *The Question Answered*, www.hawaiichristiansonline.com.

27 Quotes from Lionel Luckhoo, *The Question Answered*, www.hawaiichristiansonline.com.

Chapter 10: What are the implications of Jesus' resurrection?

1   This narrative is taken from Acts 26.4–15.

2   Dan Brown, *The Da Vinci Code* (Corgi, 2003), p. 315.

3   *The Letters of Pliny the Younger* 10.96 (Penguin Classics edition, 1969), translated by B. Radice.

4   Colossians 1.15; 2.9.

5   Titus 2.13.

6   Acts 1.9.

7   Romans 8.34; Ephesians 1.20.

8   Mark 13.24–26.

9   Acts 1:11.

10 Philippians 3.20.

11 E.g. Matthew 7.21–23.

12 John 5.30.

13 Acts 17.31.

14 Matthew 25.31–33.

15 1 Corinthians 15.20–28.

16 E.g. Romans 2.5–11.

17 E.g. Romans 8.18–21; 1 Corinthians 2.9.

18 E.g. 2 Thessalonians 1.8–9.

19 Mark 8.38.

20 2 Thessalonians 1.6–10.

21 Romans 1.21, 28.

22 John 17.3 (my italics).

23 Philippians 3.8.

24 John 14.6.

25 1 Timothy 2.5 (CEV).

26 Philippians 3.4–9 (CEV).

27 1 Timothy 1.16.

28 John 16.9.

29 Mark 7.20–23 (CEV).

30 Romans 6.23.

31 2 Thessalonians 1.8–9.

32 Ephesians 2.1 (CEV).

33 John 3.3, 8.

34 1 Timothy 1.13–14.

35 Ephesians 2.4–5 (CEV).

Chapter 11: Life from death

1 Acts 26.10–11.

2 It's clear in the gospels that there were previous plans and attempts to take Jesus' life before the one that was successful (e.g. Mark 3.6; John 8.59; 10.31). They all arose from Jesus' 'blasphemous' claims.

3 Galatians 3.13; Deuteronomy 21.23.

4 Evidence for the following summary of Jesus' innocence comes from Mark 14.55 – 15.11 and Luke 23.4–47.

5 Luke 4.1–13; John 14.31; Hebrews 4.15; 7.26; 2 Corinthians 5.21.

6 E.g. Ephesians 5.2.

7 Romans 5.8; 1 Thessalonians 5.10; Titus 2.14 (my italics).

8 2 Corinthians 5.15 (my italics).

9 John 10.14–15 (my italics).

10 John 15.13 (my italics).

11 Mark 10.45 (my italics).

12 Romans 4.25; 1 Corinthians 15.3; Galatians 1.4 (my italics).

13 2 Corinthians 5.21 (CEV).

14 Romans 8.3 (CEV).

15 2 Corinthians 5.19.

16 Matthew 26.28.

17 2 Corinthians 9.15.

18 1 Timothy 1.16 (CEV).

19 E.g. Luke 9.22; 17.25; 22.15. John reports that Jesus used the phrase 'lifted up' to foretell his death, e.g. John 3.14; 8.28; 12.32.

20 John 19.30.

21 Isaiah 53.4–6 (The Message). The rest of the poem speaks of Jesus' birth and resurrection, as well as his death. Jesus alluded to the poem as being about him, and many of the New Testament's writers quote from it – see, for example, Matthew 8.17; Luke 22.37; John 12.38; Acts 8.30–38. It's highly probable that Jesus himself helped his disciples see that it was written about him – see Luke 24.25–27, 44–47.

22 Acts 10.43; 16.31.

23 Galatians 2.20 (my italics).

24 Philippians 3.8–9 (CEV).

25 John 3.16.

26 John 5.24.

27 John 3.18.

28 Ephesians 2.4–6 (CEV).

Chapter 12: Dead or alive?

1 Luke 15.11–32.

Chapter 13: Meeting the risen Jesus

1 E.g. Mark 1.15–17.

2 Acts 26.20 (my italics).

3 Mark 8.34.

4 Romans 8.11; Ephesians 1.18–20.

5 Mark 8.35–37.

6 John 10.10.

7 Matthew 19.29.

8 Philippians 3.7–9 (CEV).

9 S. Vanauken, *Severe Mercy* (Hodder & Stoughton, 1977), p. 98.

10 See www.alpha.org or www.christianityexplored.com for more information.

11 Matthew 1.21.

12 Isaiah 55.6; Psalm 95.7–8; 2 Corinthians 6.2.

13 John 6.37.

14 John 3.16.

15 1 John 1.9 (CEV).

16 John 11.25–26.

17 John 5.24.

Postscript: What next?

1 Acts 2.41–42.
2 See www.thegoodbook.co.uk or browse in a local Christian bookshop for some examples of Bible reading notes.